Plays and Pageants for Many Occasions

by

ERNEST K. EMURIAN

Author of

Dramatized Stories of Hymns and Hymn Writers
More Dramatized Stories of Hymns and Hymn Writers

Publishers   W. A. WILDE COMPANY   Boston

331836 ♪

PLAYS AND PAGEANTS FOR MANY OCCASIONS

167

To

TRU and OODIE

PREFACE

While the facts upon which these plays are based are historically true, sufficient liberties have been taken to enhance their
dramatic value. They were written not only to provide plays for
certain occasions in school and church, but also to instruct, by
calling attention to events long neglected by the playwright, and
to inspire by linking these incidents with others of a similar
character.

Many of the plays may be presented "in part" rather than "in
whole"; they were purposely planned with this in mind. Also,
deletions of scenes or characters is allowed, where this becomes
essential, due to a shortage of available actors or a lack of adequate stage facilities.

The acts and scenes may be read aloud directly from the book
for some audiences; for others, they may be broadcast from one
room into another, as has been done successfully by several youth
groups. Every play is royalty free.

If their presentation results in a deeper appreciation of the
occasions which gave rise to certain situations depicted, or inspired the writing of hymns, songs, poems and proclamations
included, the author's purpose will be realized.

ERNEST K. EMURIAN

CONTENTS

I PLEDGE ALLEGIANCE

A PLAY

in

THREE ACTS

by

Ernest K. Emurian

This play is written so it may be given in whole or in part. Act I deals with the creation of the American flag; Act II tells, in two scenes, of Francis Bellamy and the writing of the pledge of allegiance to the flag; Act III dramatizes the origin of the Christian flag, and ties all three acts together in the conclusion.

I PLEDGE ALLEGIANCE

A Play in Three Acts

by

ERNEST K. EMURIAN

for

14 men; 2 women; Narrator; Organist and/or Pianist; Several children; Miscellaneous group of Sunday School scholars, from children to adults, as many or as few as available personnel and space will allow.

CHARACTERS

ACT   I: General George Washington
          Colonel George Ross
          Mrs. Betsy Ross
          Narrator, Organist

ACT II: Scene I; President Benjamin Harrison, 59
                  Representative Henry Cabot Lodge
                  Secretary of State Foster
                  2nd assistant secretary Brown
                  3rd assistant secretary Creidler
                  Francis Bellamy, 37
                  Organist, Narrator
          Scene II; Francis Bellamy
                  Editor James B. Upham
                  Francis Pratt, 37
                  Harold Roberts, 22
                  Organist, Narrator

ACT III: Sunday School Superintendent Charles Carlton Overton
          His assistant, John Walsh
          Sunday School secretary, Miss Alice Bennett
          Sunday School treasurer, Albert Farley
          Miscellaneous group of scholars, ranging from children to adults
          Several children to give recitations, answer and ask questions
          Flag manufacturer, Mr. Annin
          Pianist, Narrator

Stage managers for lights, curtain, make-up, etc.

11

ACT I

CHARACTERS: General George Washington, Colonel George Ross, Mrs. Betsy Ross, Narrator, Organist.
SETTING: The living room of the Ross home in Philadelphia, warmly and comfortably furnished in the fashion of the time.
TIME: One afternoon, the first week in June, 1777.

NARRATOR: No one knows just who suggested or designed the first American flag. Some attribute it to Benjamin Franklin, basing their beliefs on some remarks he made at a dinner on December 13, 1775, suggesting the adaptation of a flag after the style of one then used by the famed East India Company. The basic design of this particular banner was a series of horizontal stripes, with a specific emblem carried in the upper left hand corner. Whether this is historically true or not, we do know for a certainty that in May, 1777, Congress appointed General George Washington, Robert Morris, and Colonel George Ross to plan a flag. This scene takes place during the first week in June, 1777, just a few days after the Congressional appointment, in the living room of the Ross home in Philadelphia. General Washington is discussing the new flag with Colonel Ross and Mrs. Betsy Ross.

(*Curtain reveals scene described above.* MRS. ROSS, *with a large replica of that first flag in her hands, is seated just left of center, facing audience.* WASHINGTON *stands erectly at her right, and* COL. ROSS *at her left. They are visiting.*)

MRS. ROSS: And the thirteen stripes, General Washington, will represent the thirteen colonies.

COL. ROSS: With the same basic colors, red, white and blue, used by the British and the French in their national ensigns.

WASHINGTON: But different enough in design so as not to be confused with either of them, or with any other nation's banner, for that matter.

MRS. ROSS: Exactly, General Washington. And, as new colonies enter the Union, new stripes in alternating colors of red and white may be added at the bottom of the flag.

WASHINGTON: What if the infant republic grows beyond our dreams, to include as many as eighteen or twenty or even twenty-five colonies in the future?

COL. ROSS: That is hardly possible, General. And one or two more stripes will not appreciably alter the general lines of the new flag. Betsy, does each stripe stand for a particular colony or did you just place them in that order for no especial reason?

MRS. ROSS: Oh, no. Each stripe represents one of the thirteen colonies. Beginning with this red stripe at the top (*she points each one out as she speaks*) the red and white stripes stand for these colonies in this order: Delaware, Pennsylvania, New Jersey, Georgia, Connecticut, Massachusetts, Maryland, South Carolina, New Hampshire, Virginia, New York, North Carolina and Rhode Island.

WASHINGTON: So if any colony withdraws from our tenuous union, you will know just which stripe to eliminate!

COL. ROSS: Let us pray that that never happens, General. We are small enough now as it is; the loss of a single colony would sorely deplete our limited resources.

WASHINGTON: Well do I know that, Colonel. More than ever before we need the united support of every single colony, and of every citizen in every colony.

MRS. ROSS: The field of blue in the upper left hand corner will not be any wider than the width of the top seven stripes. Otherwise, the flag would look out of balance, a bit top-heavy, if you know what I mean.

COL. ROSS: And the white stars? They represent the thirteen colonies too, do they not?

MRS. ROSS: Yes; arranged in a circle on the field of blue they could almost remain constant through the years, while the new colonies added to the union would be symbolized by the addition of new stripes.

WASHINGTON: And if the colonies ever become too numerous we can reverse the procedure.

MRS. ROSS: How, General?

WASHINGTON: By letting the thirteen stripes represent the thirteen original colonies, and adding a new star for each additional colony.

MRS. ROSS: Excellent. The field of blue will provide ample space for fifteen or even twenty stars, as the need arises.

COL. ROSS: Then we will suggest this design to the Congress next week. Is that agreeable, General Washington?

WASHINGTON: Yes, Colonel, quite agreeable. I was asked to have the flag ready for consideration no later than June 14. Mrs. Ross, you have been most gracious and most cooperative. Our infant republic is indebted to you far beyond our feeble power to repay. Nevertheless, you may rest assured that you have made an enormous contribution to our national welfare and patriotic zeal by designing and preparing this beautiful and useful flag. Were I a minister, I could deliver a sermon right here, using this new flag as my text: The six white stripes would represent the six days of Creation, wherein God made the heavens and the earth, the sea and all that in them is.

COL. ROSS: And the seven red stripes the seven days of the week; the time God has given us in which to "glorify Him and enjoy Him."

MRS. ROSS: While the white stars shining in the field of blue represent the blue canopy of heaven under which we are all living, with the shining stars to remind us of the eternal light that shines brightest in the darkest night.

WASHINGTON: May we express the hope that this flag, this "silent symphony of red, white and blue," may ever suggest the noblest aspirations of the human soul, and fly over the infant republic as a realization of man's highest and deepest dreams of freedom, liberty, justice and peace.

(ORGANIST *plays a few strains of "America," as the* THREE CHARACTERS *hold the flag aloft, examining it in detail; and the curtain slowly closes on the scene.*)

Note: For some of this data I am indebted to "The Salute to the Flag" by my good friend, Admiral John W. W. Cumming.

ACT II

Scene 1

CHARACTERS: President Benjamin Harrison, 59; Representative Henry Cabot Lodge of Massachusetts; Secretary of State Foster; 2nd assistant, Brown; 3rd assistant, Creidler; Francis Bellamy, 37; Narrator; Organist.
SETTING: The office of the President of the United States, the White House, Washington, D.C.
TIME: Afternoon, July 21, 1892.

14

NARRATOR: Francis Bellamy was born at Mount Morris, New York, May 18, 1855, the son of David and Lucy Fells Bellamy. He spent his youthful years in the historic city of Rome, New York, located on the site of Fort Stanwix, receiving his early education in the free public schools of the city, and preparing for college at the Rome Free Academy. Though his father died when Francis was nine, he was raised by his mother with the idea of a professional career always before him. At an early age he revealed a deeply religious nature, and it was but natural that, in the choice between a career in journalism and one in the Christian ministry, he should choose the latter. Entering the University of Rochester, New York, in 1872, he graduated four years later, preparing for the ministry at the Rochester Theological Seminary. Ordination followed the completion of his seminary training, taking place in the Baptist Church at Little Falls, New York, December 1879, his twenty-fourth year. Here he served as pastor for five eventful years. Marriage to Harriet Benton of Newark, New York, came in 1881. On October 31, 1884, pastor Bellamy was called to the pastorate of Dearborn Street Baptist Church, Boston. Although the church flourished and grew under his inspired leadership, it was a shock to his congregation when he resigned in April, 1891, to enter the field of journalism. His church had this to say of him, "By his influence and inspiration, he succeeded in causing this church edifice to be planned, built and furnished. To him, not only more than any other member, but more than all of the members combined, are we indebted for our beautiful church home. While it stands, it will be a monument to the indomitable efforts of Francis Bellamy." Welcomed to the staff of the popular journal "The Youth's Companion," he was immediately appointed chairman of the executive committee for the National Public School Celebration of Columbus Day, 1892. This scene takes place in the office of Benjamin Harrison, twenty-third president of the United States, in the White House, Washington, D.C., the afternoon of July 21, 1892.

(*Curtain reveals President* HARRISON *at his desk, working over some papers, signing some, setting others aside. After a few moments, there is a knock at the door.*)

HARRISON (*looking up*): Come in. (*The door opens and*

15

ENTER *Secretary* FOSTER, *Representative* LODGE, *and* BELLAMY. *The President rises.*)

FOSTER: Mr. President, you know Mr. Lodge of Massachusetts, and Francis Bellamy of "The Youth's Companion" staff. (*They each greet him with "How do you do, Mr. President," and take chairs.*)

HARRISON: Oh, yes, I know them both quite well. In fact they were here in May, I believe, laying the ground work for the public school celebrations in connection with Columbus Day and the flag raising exercises they proposed for every school in the land.

BELLAMY: You are right, Mr. President. The same mission prompts this return visit, and we are grateful for your time and your interest.

FOSTER: You said, Mr. Bellamy, that school officials all over the country have endorsed this movement. What proof do you have to show the President other than your word, which, of course, no one questions.

BELLAMY: Mr. Foster, I have a copy of the resolutions adopted by the Superintendents of the National Educational Association at their annual meeting held in Brooklyn, and dated February 17, 1892. May I read them?

HARRISON: Please do.

BELLAMY (*reading from a document he has taken from his pocket*):

"Whereas the World's Congress Auxiliary of the World's Columbian Exposition has made a patriotic suggestion that, at the same time the Exposition grounds at Chicago are being dedicated on October 21, 1892, the Anniversary of the discovery of America, all the people of the United States unite in a celebration of the anniversary; of which celebration the public schools of the republic be everywhere in the center. Therefore, RESOLVED:

1. That the Department of Superintendents of the National Educational Association heartily endorse this suggestion, as serving the purposes both of interesting the youth of the republic in the Exposition, and also of giving to the public schools of the nation a fitting prominence as the fruit of four centuries of American life.

2. That we ask the Superintendents of Education and teachers everywhere in the republic to unite in the effort to do all in their power to make this national Columbian public school celebration both universal and successful.

3. That we request the newspaper Press of the United States to ensure the success of this celebration by lending to it the powerful aid of their sympathy and cooperation."

Two more statements follow, detailing the practical aspects of the resolution.

LODGE: The schools are behind this movement; "The Youth's Companion," the most influential journal in the land, is 100% back of it, having originated most of these outside activities.

FOSTER: And the governors of the several states; what have they done?

BELLAMY: They have already been petitioned to proclaim October 21 a holiday and most of them have already done so. In fact, of the forty-four, thirty-five have already issued proclamations, and some of the others have issued special recommendations to the same effect.

LODGE: And General Palmer, commander-in-chief of the Grand Army of the Republic, and President Grover Cleveland have both given this movement their enthusiastic endorsement.

HARRISON: Mr. Foster, ask Mr. Brown and Mr. Creidler to bring in the paper I asked them to prepare this morning.

(*Exit* FOSTER.)

HARRISON: You are a Baptist minister, are you not, Mr. Bellamy?

BELLAMY: I am, Mr. President. I've always felt a tug of war going on inside of me between the Christian ministry and the field of journalism. For some eleven years I served two different Baptist churches. Then I felt that I could serve God and my fellowmen as much through the field of journalism, which accounts for my present position with "The Youth's Companion."

HARRISON: You Baptists really get things done in this field of patriotism, don't you?

BELLAMY: What do you mean, Mr. President?

HARRISON: Wasn't it a Baptist minister in Boston who wrote "My Country 'Tis of Thee"?

17

BELLAMY: Of course. Rev. Samuel Francis Smith; he wrote it back in 1832, sixty years ago.

HARRISON: And he had the name 'Francis' too; his middle name; your first name. Quite a coincidence, isn't it.

BELLAMY: I never thought of it before. Maybe our patriotic fervor is all the more intense because of our profound and deep Christian convictions.

LODGE: Undoubtedly. The more deeply Christian our citizens become, the more enthusiastically and truly patriotic they become, in the higher and truer implications of the word.

(*Enter* FOSTER, BROWN, CREIDLER; *others rise, greet them, as* FOSTER *introduces his assistants to the others; they shake hands, exchange greetings, resume seats.*)

FOSTER: Mr. President, Mr. Brown and Mr. Creidler have completed the document.

HARRISON: Good. Mr. Creidler, you have the paper ready?

CREIDLER: Yes, Mr. President. Mr. Brown and I have been working on it for the last several hours; and it is now complete, and ready for your signature. (*He hands the document to the President who glances over it, hands it to* BROWN.)

HARRISON: Mr. Brown, let Mr. Bellamy and Mr. Lodge hear the paper, please.

BROWN (*reading the document, as* BELLAMY *and* LODGE *watch him intently with growing interest.* ORGANIST *plays very softly as background "America" and continues playing the music until the close of the scene*):

By the President of the United States of America, A Proclamation: "Whereas by a joint resolution, approved June 29, 1892, it was resolved by the Senate and the House of Representatives of the United States of America in Congress assembled, 'That the President of the United States be authorized and directed to issue a proclamation recommending to the people the observance in all their localities of the four-hundredth anniversary of the discovery of America on the twenty-first of October, eighteen hundred and ninety-two, by public demonstrations and by suitable exercises in their schools and other places of assembly';

"Now therefore I, Benjamin Harrison, President of the United States of America in pursuance of the aforesaid joint resolution

18

do hereby appoint Friday, October 21, 1892, the four-hundredth anniversary of the discovery of America by Columbus, as a general holiday for the people of the United States. On that day let the people, so far as possible, cease from toil and devote themselves to such exercises as may best express honor to the discoverer and their appreciation of the great achievements of the four completed centuries of American life.

"Columbus stood in his age as the pioneer of progress and enlightenment. The system of universal education is in our age the most prominent and salutary feature of the spirit of enlightenment, and it is peculiarly appropriate that the schools be made by the people the center of the day's demonstration. Let the National Flag float o'er every school house in the country, and the exercises be such as shall impress upon our youth the patriotic duties of American citizenship.

"In the Churches and in other places of Assembly of the people, let there be expressions of gratitude to Divine Providence for the devout faith of the discoverer, and for the Divine care and guidance which has directed our history and so abundantly blessed our people.

"In testimony whereof I have hereunto set my hand and caused the seal of the United States to be affixed.

"Done in the City of Washington, this 21st day of July, in the year of our Lord one thousand eight hundred and ninety-two and of the Independence of the United States the one-hundred and seventeenth."

"By the President: John W. Foster, Secretary of State."

(BROWN *hands document to* HARRISON; *others gather round the desk as he slowly affixes his signature to the paper.* ORGANIST *swells the music, and curtain closes on the scene.*)

See Note at end of play, regarding October 12 and October 21 dates.

ACT II

Scene 2

CHARACTERS: Francis Bellamy, 37; Editor James B. Upham, 47; Francis Pratt, 37, business manager; Harold Roberts, 22, publicity manager; Narrator; Organist.

19

SETTING: The busy office at "The Youth's Companion" where Bellamy works; 41 Temple Place, Boston; the room has the usual office period furniture, roll-top desk cluttered with papers, tables, file-cases, book shelves, chairs.

TIME: A warm evening in August, 1892.

NARRATOR: Slightly more than four weeks after Francis Bellamy visited President Benjamin Harrison in Washington, we find him back at his desk in "The Youth's Companion" building, 41 Temple Place, Boston. As the scene opens, he is re-reading final proofs of an article soon to appear in his magazine.

(*Curtain reveals scene described above.*)

BELLAMY (*reading aloud*): "Today America's fifth century begins. The world's twentieth century will soon be here. To the 13 million now in the American schools the command of the coming years belongs. We the youth of America, who today united to march as one army under the sacred flag, understand our duty. We pledge ourselves that the flag shall not be stained; and that America shall mean equal opportunity and justice for every citizen and brotherhood for the world."

(*Enter* UPHAM)

UPHAM: How goes it, Mr. Bellamy? You look tired.

BELLAMY: I am, Mr. Upham. I've been checking the proofs for the main address for Columbus Day.

UPHAM: Any corrections?

BELLAMY (*handing him the sheets*): None that I could spot.

UPHAM (*glances over the papers; goes to the door; calls*): Roberts, Roberts.

(*Enter* ROBERTS.)

ROBERTS: What is it, Mr. Upham?

UPHAM (*as* BELLAMY *resumes writing at desk*): Look over these papers and take out one or two good quotations for your Columbus Day publicity. Bellamy has some quotable material here.

ROBERTS: All right, Mr. Upham. (*He takes the papers, looks at them.*) Anything else?

UPHAM: Not now; I'll call you.

ROBERTS: I'll be in my office.

(*Exit* ROBERTS.)

UPHAM (*standing by the desk*): Bellamy, what about the salute to the flag?

BELLAMY: I thought you were going to revise the Balch salute? I tried my hand at it and it fell flat.

UPHAM: "I give my heart and my hand to my country; one country, one language, one flag."

BELLAMY: Too much repetition.

UPHAM: What do you mean?

BELLAMY: Colonel Balch used sixteen words in his salute. And in those sixteen he used the word "my" three times and the word "one" three times. That's too much repetition for so brief a statement.

UPHAM: I see. I think you are right. Could it be altered, or edited?

BELLAMY: It is really too juvenile, too childish for that.

UPHAM: True, it is. But it's something to start with. Suppose the words were re-arranged to read "My heart and my hand I give to my country."

BELLAMY: That is more poetic, but still too trite. It could apply to anyone's heart and anyone's hand—

UPHAM: And anyone's country.

BELLAMY: Exactly. There is nothing particularly American about it.

UPHAM: Too vague, or too all-inclusive. Is that your idea?

BELLAMY: Well, yes. It's too general. A salute to an American flag should say something that is typically American, without apology and without too much needless fancy phraseology.

UPHAM: Then try this, "I give my heart and my hand to America." The idea is good, but it lacks the punch—

BELLAMY: "I give my heart and my hand to America." It doesn't flow; it lacks the smooth flow that builds to a climax.

(*Enter* PRATT, *with sheaf of papers.*)

PRATT: Excuse me, Mr. Bellamy, but I have some reports for Mr. Upham.

BELLAMY: That's all right, Francis. We need a break right now.

(*Exit* BELLAMY.)

UPHAM (*looking over the papers, as* PRATT *points out details*): Circulation should be going up and this report is gratifying. Did you take care of those other matters we talked about this morning?

PRATT: Yes, Mr. Upham. And the financial statements should be ready for you by noon tomorrow.

UPHAM: Good, Mr. Pratt.

PRATT: I never knew the business manager of a magazine had so many headaches to contend with.

UPHAM: Any publisher could have told you that, young man. But you are doing a splendid job and all of us are grateful.

PRATT: As long as we stay in the black, I don't worry; it's the red ink that haunts me, to say nothing of these long hours.

UPHAM: These long hours won't last forever, Mr. Pratt. After the Columbus Day celebrations, we will all be able to relax a bit. None of us could endure for long the tension of these last few weeks.

PRATT: Let's hope it goes over with a bang. You and Mr. Bellamy have surely gone all-out to make it a success. I'll have those other papers ready in an hour. (*Leaving*) And to think I used to dream of being an editor-in-chief.

(*Exit* PRATT.)

UPHAM (*pacing the floor in deep thought*): My heart—my hand—to my flag—to my country—

(*Enter* BELLAMY.)

BELLAMY: Mr. Upham, I'm afraid we will have to set aside the Balch salute completely and start from an entirely different angle.

UPHAM: And where would you begin?

BELLAMY: Not with "my heart" or even "my country." I would stress the idea of loyalty to the flag and all that it represents.

UPHAM: Loyalty—loyalty. And then what?

BELLAMY (*sitting at the desk as* UPHAM *sits nearby*): Instead of a salute, I would begin with a vow of loyalty, a pledge, if you please—that's it, a pledge of loyalty.

UPHAM: That's good. Go on from there.

BELLAMY: A pledge of loyalty to the flag as it is being raised over 25,000 school buildings all over the land. What a theme! What a moment!

UPHAM: The crux of the entire program, Bellamy.

BELLAMY: Well do I know that, Mr. Upham. The program will stand or fall right at this point.

(Enter ROBERTS *with papers.)*

ROBERTS: Pardon another interruption, gentlemen, but I have some proofs for several pages of the final program. Would you look them over, Mr. Upham?

UPHAM *(taking the sheets, examining them)*: Mr. Roberts, balance up these parts here, and allow another inch in the margin over on this side. I believe it would look better. The rest of it seems to be all right. Check carefully for spelling and punctuation.

ROBERTS: I'll take care of that, Mr. Upham. Excuse me, gentlemen.

(Exit ROBERTS.*)*

UPHAM: Where were we, Bellamy?

BELLAMY *(looking at papers before him)*: We decided to ignore the Balch salute entirely and begin with a pledge of loyalty.

UPHAM: A pledge of loyalty. That sounds good.

BELLAMY: Better still, a pledge of allegiance.

UPHAM: Allegiance—loyalty—loyalty—allegiance. Say, you have something there, Bellamy.

BELLAMY: Allegiance sounds better; it also conveys a deeper and broader idea than the world loyalty. Don't you think so?

UPHAM: Definitely. Allegiance—that implies loyalty as well as devotion; and obedience and even service to be rendered. I like it.

(Enter PRATT.*)*

PRATT: I'm sorry to disturb you, Mr. Bellamy, but Mr. Upham has a caller. I don't know his name, Mr. Upham, but he said you gave him an appointment for this hour.

UPHAM *(rising)*: That I did, Mr. Pratt, and I forgot all about it. Bellamy, please excuse me. Now that you have gotten a start at it, I'd like for you to stay right here until you work out a clear and satisfactory formula for the salute.

BELLAMY: The "pledge," don't forget.

UPHAM: All right; the "pledge." But this is serious, Bellamy. You know it as well as I do. The entire program can rise or

23

fall on the few chosen words to be spoken by millions of school children as their—what did you call it?—their "pledge of allegiance." So work it up, if it takes all night. We are all counting on you.

BELLAMY: I'll do what I can, Mr. Upham; you know that. And I'll call you when—or if—I finish it.

UPHAM (*at the door*): Make it "when," not "if."

(*Exit* PRATT *and* UPHAM.)

BELLAMY (*walking about the room in deep thought*): I pledge allegiance—"one country, one flag, one language"—that won't do—I pledge allegiance—to the flag of my country—no —I pledge allegiance to my country's flag—to my native flag— to the flag of my nation—"my heart and my hand to my country"—those personal pronouns again—I pledge allegiance to the flag—of my country—to my flag—that's it—to *my* flag—not our flag but my flag.—I pledge allegiance to my flag —(*he hurries to his desk and writes the phrase down.* ORGAN-IST *plays hymntune "Materna" (America the Beautiful) softly until close of scene.*) I pledge allegiance to my flag—and to my nation, my country, my homeland, my democracy, my America—but which America?—the east or the west—the north or the south—Dixie or The Battle Hymn of the Republic —republic—I pledge allegiance to my flag and to the republic of America—(*he jots down the words; rises, walks about the room forming the phrases*)—And to the republic which it rep-resents—the republic it stands for—(*writes it down, tears up sheet and throws it on floor*)—to the republic for which it stands—that's it—(*writes it down; reads through the page thus far, slowly,*) I pledge allegiance to my flag and to the republic for which it stands—just what is our republic—Paul Revere's ride—Concord and Lexington—Washington at Valley Forge— John Paul Jones—"Don't give up the ship"—The Constitution and the Bill of Rights—Old Ironsides—Old North Church— "Give me liberty or give me death"—Hamilton—Jefferson— colonies becoming a country under a central government —united in war and peace—a junior choir singing "My Coun-try 'Tis of Thee"—Roger Williams in Rhode Island—Francis Asbury in Virginia—Lincoln—"the union must be preserved" —the union that cannot be dissolved, because it is of God—the union—the nation that could not be permanently severed by a bloody fraternal strife—we are one nation—undivided—"we are not divided, all one body we"—undividable—no—indivisible—that is it—we are ONE NATION INDIVISIBLE—(*He writes it down hurriedly*)—(*resumes his walking and thinking aloud*)—and what does this indivisible nation guarantee its citizens—"liberty, equality, fraternity"—the French Revolution —liberty, certainly, but hardly equality and fraternity—"we hold these truths to be self-evident; that mankind is endowed by its Creator with certain inalienable rights; that among these are life, liberty and the pursuit of happiness"—LIBERTY, the statue of liberty—the statue of freedom above the dome of the Capitol—the Supreme Court—"equal justice under law"—JUSTICE—this republic, this indivisible republic guarantees for its citizens, liberty and justice—not for one, not for a few, but for all—(*hurriedly writes down the words, reading them aloud*)—"with liberty and justice for all"—(*goes to the door; sees* PRATT *outside; calls to him*) Mr. Pratt, call Mr. Upham, please, and ask him to come to my office. Thank you (*he returns to his desk, checks over the pledge.*)

(*Enter* UPHAM.)

UPHAM: What is it, Bellamy? Do you have it?

BELLAMY (*rising, paper in hand*): I hope so, Mr. Upham.

UPHAM: Read it, please. I can hardly wait.

BELLAMY: I pledge allegiance to my flag
and to the republic for which it stands;
one nation indivisible
with liberty and justice for all.

UPHAM (*deeply moved*): Perfect—a work of genius. (*Putting his arm about* BELLAMY, *re-reading the words from the paper*) You have done the biggest thing in your life. I wish I could have done it, but I wasn't able to. You have it all right there. Others may suggest corrections or additions, but I think it is all right as it stands. This has been a great day's work. I cannot help thinking that this thing you have written will last long after you and I are dead. (*Goes to door, calls.*) Mr. Pratt, come here a moment, please. (*Enter* PRATT.) Bellamy has done it. And it is superb—a masterpiece. Read it again, Bellamy.

BELLAMY: Suppose the three of us read it together, Mr. Upham.

25

UPHAM: With our hands outstretched in tribute, palms upward, as if presenting the devotion of our hearts to the symbol of our great republic.

(*The* MEN *gather around* BELLAMY, *read the pledge from the paper, with outstretched hands, palms upward*): I pledge allegiance to my flag, and to the republic for which it stands; one nation indivisible, with liberty and justice for all.

(ORGANIST *swells the music of "America the Beautiful"; MEN lower hands, look closely at paper in* BELLAMY's *hand, and curtain closes on the scene.*)

NARRATOR: Bellamy's pledge of allegiance, and Katharine Lee Bates' hymn "America the Beautiful" were both inspired by the Chicago Columbian Exposition of 1892. It was not until the Second National Flag Conference in Washington, on Flag Day, 1924, that the pledge was changed, and the phrase "to the flag of the United States of America" substituted for the original "my flag." It is in this form that we recite Bellamy's pledge today. And, instead of saluting with outstretched arms, we place our right hands over our hearts when repeating the famous words. Author-Minister Francis Bellamy passed away in Tampa, Florida, in 1931.

ACT III

CHARACTERS: Mr. Charles Carlton Overton, Superintendent Brighton Chapel Sunday School; Assistant Supt., John Walsh; secretary, Miss Alice Bennett; treasurer, Albert Farley; Several children to recite poems, ask and answer questions; Miscellaneous group of Sunday School scholars, as many or as few as personnel and space allow; Pianist; Narrator; Flag manufacturer, Mr. Annin.

SETTING: The crowded assembly room of Brighton Chapel Sunday School, Coney Island; Rally Day; a typical gathering on a typical rally day, with all ages gathered into one room; the speakers may stand at one side, facing the audience assembled, so all may be seen and heard from the congregation; or they may stand at back of stage facing both their pupils and the congregation, but backs of scholars will then be to the audience. The side arrangement is preferable. The Sunday School officers are seated on either side of the superintendent. Pianist on piano stool, ready to play; the usual wiggling is evident; scene is one of activity and anticipation.

TIME: Sunday morning, September 26, 1897.

NARRATOR: Among the thousands of poems and hymns from the prolific pen of Fanny Crosby is one entitled "The Christian Flag," which (name) will now recite for us.

CHILD (*in front of curtain*):

The Christian flag! behold it, and hail it with a song,
And let the voice of millions the joyful strain prolong.
To every clime and nation we send it forth today;
God speed its glorious mission, with earnest hearts we pray.

The Christian flag! unfurl it, that all the world may see
The blood-stained cross of Jesus, who died to make us free.
The Christian flag! unfurl it, and o'er and o'er again
Oh, may it bear the message, "Good will and peace to men."

The Christian flag! God bless it; now throw it to the breeze,
And may it wave triumphant o'er land and distant seas,
Till all the wide creation upon its folds shall gaze,
And all the world united, our loving Saviour praise.

The Christian flag! behold it, and hail it with a song,
And let the voice of millions the joyful strain prolong.

(*Exit* CHILD)

NARRATOR: Whence came this Christian flag about which Fanny Crosby sang? Just five years after Baptist minister Francis Bellamy composed the Pledge of Allegiance to the flag of the United States of America, on Sunday morning, September 26, 1897, to be exact, Rally Day was being observed at Brighton Chapel Sunday School, Coney Island, New York. The superintendent, Mr. Charles Carlton Overton, had invited a prominent Christian layman to be the special speaker for the occasion. The little chapel was crowded to capacity for the exercises that morning. This scene takes place just before the expected arrival of the guest speaker. Superintendent Overton is speaking to an assembly of Sunday School scholars, officers and teachers.

(*Curtain reveals the scene described above.*)

OVERTON: Boys and girls—boys and girls—let me have your attention, please. (*They gradually quiet down and listen.*) On behalf of Brighton Chapel Sunday School we welcome each and every one of you to our Rally Day program. In addition to the usual Rally Day exercises, we have planned a special treat for all of you. A prominent Christian layman from New York accepted my invitation to be present with us this morning and bring an address appropriate to the occasion. We expect him to arrive at any moment. In the meantime, I'm going to ask our pianist to play, while the smaller children from the Beginner and Primary departments sing the children's universal favorite, "Jesus Loves Me."

(PIANIST *plays and the smaller children sing a verse or two, with chorus, of "Jesus Loves Me," after which the others applaud vigorously.*)

OVERTON: I wonder if the Juniors and the Intermediates and Seniors have a special hymn they would like to sing for the rest of us at this time.

JUNIOR BOY: Let's sing "Brightly Gleams Our Banner." (*Others show approval; "That's good," "All right," nodding their heads.*)

OVERTON: Good. "Brightly Gleams Our Banner" it will be. (PIANIST *plays; the older boys and girls sing a couple of stanzas. During their singing,* OVERTON *talks anxiously with the other officers, goes to door looking for speaker; returns, whispers to* WALSH; *consults, talks with secretary and treasurer in whispers. Following the singing,* MR. OVERTON *rises and speaks.*)

OVERTON: Good, boys and girls, good. I cannot imagine what is delaying our speaker. Suppose we hear a word from our assistant superintendent, Mr. John Walsh.

WALSH (*rising, standing before the assembly*): Thank you, Mr. Overton. Sunday School students, officers and teachers, this is undoubtedly the finest Rally Day attendance we have ever enjoyed here at Brighton Chapel. It is a tribute to our splendid superintendent and faithful corps of teachers and all of their assistants and helpers. I am sure I am expressing the sentiments of everyone present when I tell our teachers that we are indebted to them more deeply than we can either express or attempt to repay for their devotion to their classes, for their faithful attendance Sunday after Sunday and for their sincere interest in the spiritual welfare of every student in every Sunday School class. As assistant superintendent, I have little enough to do, but we can never magnify too highly the office of Sunday School teacher. We commend all of you, and will continue to work with you, pray for you and support you in every way during the coming year as we have tried to do during the year that has just closed. Now, let us have a brief report from our efficient secretary, Alice Bennett.

MISS BENNETT (*rising, holding a large book in her hand*): Mr. Walsh, I haven't figured out all of the percentages accurately yet. Would you let me hold my report until the close of the assembly?

WALSH: Surely, Miss Bennett. Can we have a word from our treasurer, Mr. Farley?

FARLEY (*consulting his book, rising*): Mr. Walsh, our offerings during the past year have enabled us to meet all bills when they were due, including utilities and literature, picnics and parties, and one or two small emergencies that arose unexpectedly. In addition we sent a considerable amount to the mission board for the partial support of a foreign missionary; and we are reporting a balance in the general Sunday School treasury of $65.32.

WALSH (*as* OVERTON *continues to walk back to the door, and to the front of the room, pacing anxiously, looking for the speaker*): Thank you, Mr. Farley. Not many of our students know this, but the work of a Sunday School secretary and treasurer is a job involving many hours work each week. Things run smoothly on Sundays because of the back-stage work given freely and gladly by many of our officers. We are grateful to each one of them. Thank you both.

OVERTON (*returning to the front*): Boys and girls, let's sing another hymn. I'm sure our speaker will be here in a few minutes. I cannot understand his delay. But it is just one of those things that usually happen on special days. And Rally Day is no exception. Try "Onward, Christian Soldiers."

(PIANIST *plays and all join in singing several stanzas of "Onward, Christian Soldiers."*)

WALSH (*rising*): Boys and girls, and all of you who are members and friends of our Sunday School, as well as the visitors and strangers here with us this morning, our speaker has not yet arrived. In that case, there is only one thing to do;

29

that is to call upon our able, energetic and capable Sunday School Superintendent, Mr. Overton, to bring us a few remarks. (*The children applaud.* OVERTON *takes his place before them, stands quietly until applause ceases.*)

OVERTON: Boys and girls, young people and adults, this is rather embarrassing for me, I assure you. I cannot understand what has happened to prevent our speaker from arriving. But he isn't here; that's certain. Because if he were, I wouldn't be up here trying to improvise an appropriate speech on the spur of the moment. (*He glances casually about the room, spies the large American flag draped over one corner of the pulpit. Points to it.*) Do you remember the hymns you have been singing? What are they? Who can recall?

CHILDREN: "Brightly Gleams Our Banner," "Onward, Christian Soldiers," "Jesus Loves Me."

OVERTON (*motioning for silence*): That's right. And the first two hymns had something in common. Who can tell me what it was?

CHILD: "Brightly Gleams Our Banner" is about a banner waving before God's hosts.

CHILD: "Waving On Christ's Soldiers to Their Home on High."

CHILD: And "Onward, Christian Soldiers" is about "the cross of Jesus going on before." Is that right?

OVERTON: Correct, children. They refer to a Christian banner waving before God's army, and a cross that goes on before as we battle for Him against the forces of evil. But, tell me. What banner do our armies use when they march into battle?

BOY: The American flag.

OVERTON: You're right, son. The banner of our great nation is the beloved American flag.

BOY: And is the banner of the Church a Christian flag, Mr Overton?

OVERTON: It should be, son. In fact, that's the theme of my talk this morning: The Christian flag. (*He holds up the American flag for all to see.*) See this American flag. Notice how it is arranged, with stars and stripes in one place, representing the thirteen original colonies from which our nation sprung; and the white stars on a field of blue stand for the separate states of the union. Now, while the British and French flags have the same colors, they would never be mistaken for this flag, would they?

CHILDREN: No; no. The lines are different; they're put together different.

OVERTON: That's right; they are put together differently. The Christian flag, though, should represent Christian people in all countries, shouldn't it?

CHILDREN: Yes; yes (*nod approvingly*).

OVERTON: So we will let this Christian flag, which we are fashioning for the first time here this morning, remind every person everywhere of his allegiance to God, just as the American flag reminds us of our allegiance to the United States of America. We will make the main body of the flag white in color. White stands for purity, and innocence and peace.

CHILD: Is that why girls wear white when they get married?

OVERTON: Why, yes. The white bridal dress and veil symbolize purity and innocence. White has been the symbol of peace for countless generations. Tell me, what is the color of a flag of truce when nations are at war?

BOY: It's a white flag; and it can be a piece of a shirt or a sheet or just anything white.

OVERTON: When the enemy sees the man bearing this white flag of truce, they stop their shooting, to talk over peace terms with the other delegation. So the main field of the Christian flag should be white. And over in this corner (*pointing to the stars in the American flag*) corresponding to the place of the white stars in the nation's flag, I propose a smaller field of deep blue, since blue is the color of the unclouded sky, and a symbol of faith, trust and sincerity. What do you call someone who has proven faithful to you, or refused to lose his trust in you?

BOY: True-blue.

OVERTON: Exactly. Because blue stands for sincerity and truth and constancy and faith. And emblazoned in red on this field of blue will be the cross, the symbol of the Saviour's death and subsequent triumph over death.

OLDER GIRL: That's red, white and blue, just like the American flag, isn't it?

31

OVERTON: Yes; the very same colors, but arranged in a different way, and representing different truths. This is our Christian flag, the banner which is floating o'er us, and going on before us as, in Christ's Name, we seek to win the world for God. (*He consults his watch.*) Children, our time is over. I regret that our expected speaker did not arrive, but I want to thank you for helping me improvise a new banner, the Christian flag. Who knows? Maybe here this morning we started something that will greatly enrich the life of the Church in the years that lie ahead. Maybe our conception of a Christian flag was God's providential way of overruling our disappointment for His own glory. As we close, let us rise and sing our closing hymn, "God Be With You Till We Meet Again."

(*All rise, find the place, smile to one another and nod.* OVERTON *looks again at the familiar stanzas, smiles, motions for silence.*)

OVERTON: I had forgotten the phrase in the fourth stanza, but the lines are most appropriate with which to close our program this morning.

> "God be with you till we meet again,
> Keep love's banner floating o'er you."

Let us sing the first and fourth stanzas in closing.

(PIANIST *plays and* ALL *sing the first and fourth stanzas of* "*God Be With You.*" *As they sing the final chorus, the curtain closes on the scene.*)

MR. ANNIN (*with Christian flag in his hand, enters, stands center, front of curtain*): My name is Annin. It's an unusual name, spelled A N N I N. I am known as a manufacturer of flags. Mr. Overton was so enthused over his idea for a Christian flag that he came to me the week following his impromptu address at Brighton Chapel Sunday School. I immediately caught his enthusiasm and helped him fashion the first Christian flag. We made it exactly as he had originally described it, with a large field of white; a smaller field of blue, with the cross of Jesus emblazoned on it in bright red. And today I am assisting him in spreading this message far and wide throughout Christendom, and bending my efforts to secure its wide adoption. In

32

closing, let me narrate one of the thrilling stories that will always come to my mind when I see a Christian flag.

(ENTIRE CAST *assembles on stage standing about* MR. ANNIN, *during a brief pause; they all watch him intently as he tells this closing story.* BELLAMY *carries a large American flag with him.*)

Bishop George Washington Doane was an honored Episcopalian clergyman. He founded the famous girls school, St Mary's on the Delaware, at Burlington, New Jersey. His campus home was named "Riverside." One evening in December, 1848, he and his two sons were visiting in the study at "Riverside," when one of the boys looked out across the river, and, to his surprise, saw a church building floating down the river. Looking closer, the three men saw that the church was on a big barge, being towed down the river toward Philadelphia. Later they learned that it was truly a floating house of worship built especially for the Philadelphia Sailors' Mission. One of the boys spotted a banner or flag waving from the steeple, but, in the gathering darkness, could not make out just what kind of a banner or flag it was. But Bishop Doane saw a quick connection between a banner atop a church steeple and a flag-raising ceremony scheduled for St. Mary's the very next week. Finding this inspiration almost made to order, he composed the thrilling stanzas entitled "Fling out the banner." Although he wrote the hymn almost half a century prior to Mr. Overton's Christian flag, nevertheless his hymn can well apply to the Christian banner which he envisioned then, but did not see. (*He holds aloft the Christian flag;* ORGANIST *plays hymntune "Doane," while various children recite the stanzas of Bishop Doane's famous hymn.*)

CHILD: Fling out the banner! Let it float
Skyward and seaward, high and wide;
The sun that lights its shining folds,
The cross on which the Saviour died.

2nd CHILD: Fling out the banner! Angels bend
In anxious silence o'er the sign;
And vainly seek to comprehend
The wonder of the love divine.

33

(BELLAMY *holds aloft the American Flag; a* BOY *and* GIRL *step to the front, salute, and recite the pledge, "I pledge allegiance to the flag of the United States of America, and to the republic for which it stands; one nation, indivisible, with liberty and justice for all." They step back to their places.*)

3rd CHILD: Fling out the banner! Heathen lands
Shall see from far the glorious sight,
And nations, crowding to be born,
Baptize their spirits in its light.

4th CHILD: Fling out the banner! Sin-sick souls
That sink and perish in the strife,
Shall touch in faith its radiant hem,
And spring immortal into life.

(ANNIN *holds aloft the Christian flag; a* BOY *and* GIRL *step forward; place right hand over heart, repeat the pledge, "I pledge allegiance to the Christian flag, and to the Saviour for whose Kingdom it stands; one brotherhood, uniting all mankind in service and in love." (A.E.Av and F.K.S.) They step back into places.*)

5th CHILD: Fling out the banner! Let it float
Skyward and seaward, high and wide;
Our glory only in the cross;
Our only hope, the Crucified!

6th CHILD: Fling out the banner! Wide and high,
Seaward and skyward let it shine;
Nor skill, nor might, nor merit our's.
We conquer only in that sign.

(ENTIRE CAST *sings, as* ORGANIST *plays, the first stanza of "Fling Out the Banner."* BELLAMY *may, if appropriate, invite the assembled congregation or audience to rise and unite in the singing.* CAST *may either remain on stage for curtain after the singing, or may walk slowly offstage during singing, with audience dismissed by prayer or benediction.*)

The End

Note: With the exception of Overton and Annin, the characters in Act III are entirely fictional. The facts upon which this play is based are true; but the development of them in the various scenes is imaginary. The play may be presented in whole or in part, depending upon available characters in local situations.

Note: In Act II, Scene 1, The Presidential Proclamation gives the date October 21; the original Columbus Day was actually October 12. The change in the world's calendars during the intervening four hundred years called for an adjustment of nine days; hence the other date for the Chicago celebration. This apparent difficulty was resolved, and a later Congressional bill set aside October 12 as Columbus, or Discovery Day.

The material on which the Act is based comes from the book "I Pledge Allegiance" by Margarette S. Miller of Portsmouth, Va., the complete history of Bellamy and his famous pledge. I am indebted to her for permission to use this data from her excellent book.

Ernest K. Emurian

'TWAS THE NIGHT BEFORE CHRISTMAS

A PLAY
in
ONE ACT

Dramatizing the true story of the writing of this famous poem

by

Ernest K. Emurian

'TWAS THE NIGHT BEFORE CHRISTMAS

A Play

by

ERNEST K. EMURIAN

for: 4 men, 1 woman, 1 boy, 2 small children, group of children, Musician, Assistants

CHARACTERS

REV. CLEMENT CLARKE MOORE, 43; dignified Seminary professor.
His wife, CATHARINE.
Their seven-year-old son, CLARKE. (Since an older boy would be able to play the part more effectively, the age of the one to take this part is left to the discretion of the director.)
PHYSICIAN
PROFESSOR JACKSON, a neighbour and friend.
TWO TINY ANGELS
GROUP OF CHILDREN, playmates, ages from 6 to 12.
NARRATOR
OFFSTAGE VOICES
ORGANIST OR MUSICIAN (with chimes, bells)
STAGE MANAGERS
SETTING: A typical boy's bedroom; the bed is a bit left center; table, chairs, dressers, lamps, rugs, stove or fireplace, complete the warm atmosphere of the room. The door may be to left or right, with a window near head of bed against back wall. The costumes and interior are typical of eastern United States, 1822.
TIME: Christmas Eve, 1822.

NARRATOR: Rev. Clement Clarke Moore was born in Chelsea, New York, July 15, 1779, the son of Rev. Benjamin Moore and Charity Clarke, daughter of Major Thomas Clarke. Attending Columbia College, he graduated in 1798. Although his father wanted him to take Holy Orders, young Clement decided to be a good Christian layman instead. On November 20, 1813, he married Catharine Elizabeth Taylor. Following his father's death, Clement found himself doing more Church work and engaging in more religious activities. Having inherited his father's estate, on February 1819, through Bishop Hobart, he donated sixty lots in New York City, including the site known as Chelsea Square, on condition that the buildings of a theological seminary be erected thereon. In 1821 he became professor of Biblical Learning and Interpretation of Scripture in the Diocesan Seminary erected on the land he had recently given for that purpose. Here he was to remain for more than a quarter of a century. This scene takes place in a bedroom of the Moores' New York City home, the early evening of Christmas Eve, 1822.

(*Curtain reveals scene described above.*)

MRS. MOORE (*offstage, anxiously*): Bring him in here, Clement. (*Enter* MRS. MOORE *in a great hurry; she straightens up the bed, placing an old blanket over the quilt. Enter* MR. MOORE *carying son* CLARKE *in his arms; the boy is dressed for the out-of-doors; but his coat, hat, boots are muddy; he is moaning in great pain.*)

CLARKE: My pony—my pony—what happened to my pony? —(*He breaks down and cries, as* MR. MOORE *lays him gently on the bed, and begins to take off his heavy winter clothes, soothing and comforting the lad.*)

MR. MOORE: You'll be all right, son; daddy's here—mother's here; let me help you get your coat off. Catharine, help him with his boots. (*She begins taking off the left boot. Boy cries in pain.*)

CLARKE: My leg—mother—be careful—it hurts. (*Parents cast frightened glances at each other*)—careful, mother—it hurts—I've broken my leg—and I killed my pony—I've broken my leg—and I've killed my pony—

MR. MOORE: Catharine, call the physician. I'll get his boots off; and don't worry, dear; he isn't the first boy who has broken a leg. I know it hurts, but I don't think it's critical.

MRS. MOORE (*going to head of bed, rubbing lad's forehead*): You're going to be all right, Clarke. I'm going to call the doctor while daddy gets your heavy things off. Try to lie quietly. If your leg is broken, try not to move it. Mother loves you; you know that. And we're going to do everything we can to relieve your pain and make you well again.

40

(*Exit* Mrs. Moore.)

Mr. Moore (*continuing to help the lad remove his winter clothes, boots*): Don't worry about your pony, Clarke. We can always get another pony. It's *you* we're worried about right now. We want you to be all right for Christmas. I'm going to get some warm water and a wash cloth and get some of this mud off. Lie carefully and I'll be right back. (*Exit* Mr. Moore, *to re-enter in a moment, with a basin of warm water, wash cloth, towel. He takes off his coat, throws it over a chair, washes off the mud from the boy's face, hands, as they continue conversation.*)

Clarke: My pony—did they *have* to shoot him, daddy? Couldn't they have put a splint on his leg? Did they have to shoot him?

Mr. Moore: They don't usually put splints on animals, son. Their bones are too thin—too brittle; and they won't lie still like boys will.

Clarke: Will the doctor put a splint on my leg, daddy?

Mr. Moore: If it's broken, he'll have to.

Clarke: And I'll have to stay in bed on Christmas? Oh, daddy—no—

Mr. Moore: I'm afraid so, Clarke; but let's be thankful it was no worse than it was. When our neighbour ran over and told us about the accident, mother and I imagined the worst.

Clarke: Why?

Mr. Moore: That's just the way parents are, son. And when I saw you lying there—and all that blood on the white snow —my heart sank.

Clarke: Most of the blood came from my pony, daddy. It wasn't all *my* blood.

Mr. Moore: I know it now, but I didn't know it when we first saw you.

Clarke: Poor pony—poor pony—lying there, kicking and crying—and I couldn't do anything to help him—he was a nice pony, daddy.

Mr. Moore: A very nice pony, son—one of the nicest I've ever seen.

Clarke: He was so gentle—so kind—he wouldn't hurt anybody, daddy. I didn't know the road was covered with ice

41

—if I had, we would have turned around and come back home.

MR. MOORE: Those things happen so quickly—and icy roads are so treacherous—it is all over before you know it. (CLARKE *covers his face with his hands and weeps.*) I'm sorry, son. I know how much you loved your pony. (*He places basin and towels etc. on nearby stand, sits by head of bed, his arm about his boy.*) As soon as you are up and about we'll go down to the stable and buy a new pony.

(*Enter* MRS. MOORE *and* PHYSICIAN. MR. MOORE *rises to greet them; they take off wraps and* PHYSICIAN *goes over to examine the lad, greeting him cheerfully by name.*)

CLARKE: Hello, doctor. Will it hurt?

PHYSICIAN (*sympathetically, smiling*): How do I know, young fellow? I haven't examined you yet.

CLARKE: But daddy and mother said my leg was broken. Will it hurt?

PHYSICIAN: If the bone is broken, then most of the hurting is over. I'll put your leg in a cast and let it stay until the broken parts grow together again.

CLARKE: And it won't hurt?

PHYSICIAN: (*feeling the leg*): I don't think so, son. But your father and mother were right. It seems to be broken right below the knee. (MR. *and* MRS. MOORE *stand nearby, watching; his arm about her, steadying her.*) Tell me what happened, Clarke. From the looks of things you had a pretty bad time of it.

MR. MOORE: You should have seen him before we got his muddy clothes off and before I washed the dirt off his face and hands.

MRS. MOORE: Is he badly hurt, doctor?

PHYSICIAN: Not too badly, Mrs. Moore. His left leg is broken, like I said, but it's a clean break, one that ought to mend quickly.

CLARKE: Will I be able to eat Christmas dinner, doctor?

PHYSICIAN (*laughing*): If you are well enough to start worrying about Christmas dinner, you'll recover. A healthy appetite is a good sign, young fellow. But about the accident—what happened?

CLARKE: I was out with my sled and my pony; we had ridden

down the street a couple of blocks and turned around and were going up the other way.

PHYSICIAN: At a walk or a trot?

CLARKE: Well, you know how it is—

MR. MOORE: That means "at a gallop," doctor.

MRS. MOORE: And in all this ice and snow.

PHYSICIAN: Go ahead, Clarke. You were going up the street at a gallop—

CLARKE: And all of a sudden my pony slipped up on the ice and before I knew it the sled was turning over on top of me and my pony was lying there on the snow, kicking and crying and I could feel blood on my face and hands—

PHYSICIAN (*fixing a splint on the left leg*): You're a lucky boy, Clarke. Maybe the very fact that your pony broke his leg when he fell saved your life.

CLARKE: What do you mean? (MR. MOORE *assists with splint as* MRS. MOORE *sits nearby.*)

PHYSICIAN: If the sled had turned suddenly when the pony slipped, and then the pony had gotten to his feet again, he could have dragged you underneath the sled, and there's no telling what would have happened.

MRS. MOORE: Oh, no; it's too terrible.

PHYSICIAN: So the fact that your pony broke his leg saved you from more serious injury.

CLARKE: But they shot him, doctor—they shot him.

PHYSICIAN: I know, Clarke; your father told me. There was nothing else to do. There was really nothing else to do. It put him out of his misery quickly; it was the most merciful thing to do under the circumstances.

CLARKE: I know; but it seems awful—to shoot a poor pony—

PHYSICIAN (*completing his work*): That's got it, young fellow. Now lie quietly, and stay right here in bed. I'll come back later this evening and prepare a cast; the splint will hold your leg straight and keep the broken bones in position until I return. Now be a good boy and do what I say; and you'll be jumping around here in no time at all. (PHYSICIAN *takes* MR. MOORE *by the arm and the two men Exit.* MRS. MOORE *sits down on edge of bed, strokes lad's forehead.*)

MRS. MOORE: I'm sorry about your pony, Clarke. But daddy promised we would get another one as soon as you are able to be up and about again.

CLARKE: I know, mother. But when I think of what happened I just want to curl up somewhere and die; I feel so alone —so all by myself.

MRS. MOORE: But you're not; we're here with you.

(*Offstage, children's voices heard, singing "O Come All Ye Faithful." Lights in room gradually dim.*)

CLARKE: It's the children—out carolling—

MRS. MOORE: They're singing "O Come All Ye Faithful."

CLARKE: And I wanted to go with them—oh, why did all this have to happen—

MRS. MOORE: Let's sing the chorus with them. (*She begins singing chorus, "O come let us adore him" and sings it to the end. Children offstage begin second stanza.*)

CLARKE: I don't want to adore anything. I don't feel like singing.

MRS. MOORE (*lovingly*): I know, son. (*She places a blanket over him; they listen to the children singing the last stanza and chorus, and voices disappear in the distance. CLARKE closes his eyes and soon is sleeping. Lights are dimmer. MRS. MOORE lights a lamp nearby, turning it low. Exit MRS. MOORE. CLARKE tosses in his sleep. Enter MR. MOORE; he picks up a book; sits in nearby rocker by the lamp reading quietly. A short while later, enter MRS. MOORE with a group of children, playmates, aged 6 to 12.*)

MRS. MOORE (*motioning to the children to be quiet*): Clement, some of Clarke's playmates are here. Is he asleep? (*The children stand silently just inside the door. MR. MOORE goes over to the bed.*)

MR. MOORE: I think so. (*He looks at the lad, who stirs.*)

CLARKE: What is it, daddy?

MR. MOORE: Some of your playmates came over to see you. (*To the children*): You can come in for a few moments; he's had a pretty bad accident and needs a lot of rest.

(*The children gather by the bedside, greeting their playmate by name.*)

CHILD: Did you break your leg, Clarke?

CLARKE (*nodding*): Yes; I did; and the doctor put a splint on it.

CHILD: Will they have to shoot you, too?

MR. MOORE: Why, no, sonny. They shoot horses and ponies because their leg bones are so long and thin it is almost impossible to put them in a cast so they can mend and heal and grow together. But they don't shoot little boys.

MRS. MOORE: Or little girls, for that matter. Clarke has a splint on his left leg, holding the broken parts in place until the doctor can put a cast on it.

ANOTHER CHILD: We're sorry, Clarke; about you and the pony.

ANOTHER CHILD: We're going carolling after a while, Clarke; do you want us to stop by and sing for you?

MRS. MOORE: We heard you singing "O Come All Ye Faithful" a little while ago. It was beautiful. I think it would be lovely if you stopped out on the lawn just below the window and sang again on your way home.

CLARKE: I'd like it.

CHILD: Then we'll do it for you; we promise.

ANOTHER CHILD: Will Santa Claus come to see you if you're sick in bed?

CLARKE: I hope so. Will he, daddy?

MR. MOORE: Of course he will, son. (*To his wife*) Catharine, don't we have some Christmas candy we can share with the children?

MRS. MOORE: Of course we have. I forgot all about it. Just a minute, children. (*Exit* MRS. MOORE, *returning and passing the candy bowl to the children, who help themselves.*)

CHILD: Is there really a Santa Claus, Mr. Moore?

CHILD: I think there is, but my brother told me there wasn't any such thing.

MR. MOORE: Children, if you'll sit down here on the floor, I'll tell you about a real Santa Claus, and you can figure it all out for yourselves.

CHILD (*as the children sit down about the room*): Was he big and fat?

ANOTHER CHILD: Did he wear a red suit?

ANOTHER CHILD: And what about his big bundles of toys?

45

Mr. Moore: That remains to be seen. But this story is a true story. Way back, hundreds of years ago, in the fourth century of the Christian era—

Child: What does that mean?

Mr. Moore (*smiling*): It means that this story happened a long, long time ago. Now let me start all over again. A long, long time ago there lived a very good man. His name was Nicholas and he was a bishop of the church.

Child: What's a bishop?

Mr. Moore: Some good Episcopalian ought to know.

Another Child: I know; he is a preacher who is over a lot of other preachers.

Another Child: My daddy says a bishop is a headache!

Mr. Moore (*laughing*): Some bishops may cause headaches, sonny, but most of them are noble Christian gentlemen. And a bishop is in charge of many churches just as a regular minister is in charge of one church. He has the oversight of these churches, to help them, advise them, lead them—

Child: And to confirm the children.

Mr. Moore: Exactly. That's one of his most important duties. Now this Bishop Nicholas lived in the town of Myra, in Asia Minor. That's thousands of miles from here, but not very far from the land of Palestine where Jesus lived and taught. He was a good man, who was deeply interested in all of his people. In fact, he took the gold that was given to him and had a goldsmith melt it down and re-fashion it in such a way that everyone would know the money belonged to Bishop Nicholas.

Child: What did the man do with the gold?

Mr. Moore: Well, the goldsmith melted the money down and fashioned it into three gold balls. (*Enter* Professor Jackson, *standing in dark just inside the door; no one sees him.*)

Clarke: What did he do with the gold balls, daddy?

Mr. Moore: He spent it for other people. If a man was taken into slavery, he bought him back with a gold ball; if a widow needed food or clothing for her family, he gave her a gold ball with which to buy them. And the store-keepers all knew that the gold ball belonged to Bishop Nicholas and had to be returned to him, so he could spend it for someone else who was in need. Someone even built a church and paid for it with a gold ball. Soon people all over that part of the world knew of Bishop Nicholas and his three gold balls. Someone even made a sign out of three make-believe gold balls and hung it over the door to Bishop Nicholas' office, so people everywhere would know where to go for help.

PROFESSOR (*stepping into the room*): Three gold balls, brother Moore? Don't tell me you're thinking of pawning your gifts *before* Christmas.

MR. MOORE (*rising, greeting his friend*): Why, no, Professor. I was telling the children about the first Saint Nicholas, and his three gold balls. (*He introduces* PROFESSOR JACKSON *to the children.*)

PROFESSOR: Strange, isn't it, how that thing began. And now instead of hanging over doors to churches, the sign of three gold balls hangs over pawn shops, where people take the gifts they didn't want to pawn them for money to pay for gifts they gave to other people that possibly they didn't want!

MR. MOORE: What a let down from Bishop Nicholas! (*To the children*): Well, children, *he* was the original Santa Claus; the first Saint Nicholas; an honest to goodness Christian minister. But I think it is time you children got on with your carolling. It's late, and you will want to be home before it gets too cold. Stop by tomorrow, if you can. I'm sure Clarke will be glad to see you. (*Exit the children, turning and wishing Clarke a "Merry Christmas" as they leave; he, in turn, extends to them the familiar greetings.*)

PROFESSOR (*going over to the bed*): I'm sorry about what happened, Clarke. If there is anything we can do for you over at our house, please let us know; the girls send their love.

CLARKE (*weakly*): Thank you, Mr. Jackson. Emily is going to miss the pony almost as much as I.

PROFESSOR: I know that, Clarke; she loved the pony dearly.

MR. MOORE (*feeling the lad's forehead*): He has a little fever, I think. Does he feel hot to you?

PROFESSOR (*laying his hand on the forehead*): A little; yes.

MR. MOORE: The doctor promised to stop by again.

PROFESSOR: Then I'm sure he will prescribe something for the fever.

(*Enter* Mrs. Moore *with a bowl of soup.*)

Mrs. Moore: Oh, Professor Jackson. I didn't hear you come in.

Professor: I saw footprints of children in the snow, and the front door was unlocked; so I just came on in.

Mrs. Moore: That was thoughtful of you. Let me give Clarke some soup and I'll fix a pot of coffee for you men.

Mr. Moore (*taking the bowl*): I'll feed him, Catharine, if you will prepare the coffee.

Mrs. Moore: Fine. I'll be back with the coffee in a few minutes. (*Exit* Mrs. Moore. Mr. Moore *sits by the bed, feeding the lad;* Professor *sits in a rocker nearby.*)

Clarke: Daddy, was that Bishop Nicholas really the first Santa Claus?

Mr. Moore (*feeding him the soup*): His name was Nicholas, son; and when the Church canonized him—

Clarke: Did what to him?

Professor: You're not teaching college graduates, Clement.

Mr. Moore: You're right; I'm not. I've spoken to them so much I've almost forgotten how to talk to children. But when Bishop Nicholas died, the leaders of the Church proclaimed or declared him a saint, and people spoke of him as Saint Nicholas. Later the children heard of his good deeds, especially at Christmas time, and shortened his name to St. Nick.

Professor: And it was the Dutch, I believe, who took the idea of St. Nick and came out with a Santa Claus of their very own.

Mr. Moore: Jan, the old Dutchman, was telling me about it just yesterday when I met him at the store. I was waiting for the turkey we had ordered, and the old man helped me pass the time by repeating the fairy tales of their Santa Claus, and his tiny reindeer who flew through the skies on Christmas Eve, giving toys to good little girls and boys all over the world.

Professor: Interesting legend. Jan himself could fill the bill, with his rosy cheeks and his chubby build, to say nothing of his luxuriant white beard.

Mr. Moore: A perfect picture, even to his stubby pipe and the habit he has of placing his finger aside of his nose when he is deep in thought.

48

CLARKE: I've had enough, daddy. I'm hot; get me a drink of water.

MR. MOORE (*feeling the lad's forehead*): All right, son. (*To* PROFESSOR): Look after him. I'll be right back. (*Exit* MR. MOORE, *reappearing in a few moments with a glass of water. The lad drinks it, and then sinks back on his pillow, exhausted. Enter* MRS. MOORE *with coffee for the two men. They resume their seats, and sip the coffee. She goes over to the bed, feels the boy's forehead; looks about anxiously.*)

MRS. MOORE: He feels feverish. I'm worried.

MR. MOORE: There's nothing we can do until the doctor returns.

PROFESSOR: Shall I go for him?

MR. MOORE: I don't think that's necessary. He promised to come back as soon as he could.

MRS. MOORE: I hope he comes before too long. I don't like this high fever.

PROFESSOR (*placing cup and saucer on nearby dresser, rising*): If there is nothing I can do to help, I'd better be going. There's a little matter of decorating a Christmas tree.

MR. MOORE (*rising*): I had completely forgotten about our tree.

MRS. MOORE: Why don't we bring the tree in here, Clement. I know Clarke will enjoy watching us decorate it.

MR. MOORE (*accompanying the* PROFESSOR *to the door*): That's good. I'll do it right now.

(*Exit* PROFESSOR *and* MR. MOORE.)

(MRS. MOORE *busies herself straightening up the bed and the room, picking up coffee cups. Exit* MRS. MOORE *as the lad sleeps. A few moments later enter* MR. *and* MRS. MOORE *with a small Christmas tree and box of assorted decorations. They place the tree near the bed, and begin decorating it. After a few minutes, while they work quietly, the doorbell rings.*)

MRS. MOORE: I hope it is the doctor.

MR. MOORE (*going to answer the door*): It's a bit early for him, I'm afraid. (*Exit* MR. MOORE. OFFSTAGE VOICES *are heard.* MR. MOORE *calls to his wife offstage*): Catharine. (*He comes to the door*): Catharine, Mr. and Mrs. Black are here. Can you come out a moment?

49

MRS. MOORE: Why, yes. (*Exit* MRS. MOORE, *after turning lamp down low. Hushed voices heard offstage.*)

(ORGAN *plays "Silent Night" very softly, on chimes if possible. Two* TINY ANGELS *enter very softly; they proceed to decorate the tree.* CLARKE *wakens suddenly, looks up, sees them, stares, then lies back in a fitful sleep.* ANGELS *continue decorating tree and then quietly exit as* ORGANIST *plays the tune for second or third time, slowly.*)

OFFSTAGE VOICES: MR. MOORE: Good night, and thank you for coming.

OFFSTAGE: MRS. MOORE: And a Merry Christmas to you and your family; goodnight.

(*Enter* MR. *and* MRS. MOORE, *with holly and other room decorations. As they place them about the room,* CLARKE *wakens, sees them, sits up excitedly.*)

CLARKE: Daddy—mother, do you know what I saw? Two little angels—right here in my room—

MRS. MOORE (*rushing to his side; feeling his forehead*): Now, darling; you're sick; you're just imagining things.

CLARKE: No, I'm not, mummy. I know a little angel when I see one; and there were two little angels right here in my room, decorating the Christmas tree. Daddy, what does that mean?

MR. MOORE: I don't know, son—I don't know.

CLARKE: Does it mean that I'm going to die and go to heaven and be an angel?

MRS. MOORE (*sitting on bedside*): No, precious. It means that God wants you to get well and strong again so you can be our little angel right here on earth.

CLARKE: Oh, I thought they came to take me with them. (*He falls back on pillow, and closes his eyes.*)

MRS. MOORE: I'm worried. The poor lad is out of his head. (*Enter* PHYSICIAN *quietly.*)

PHYSICIAN (*as* MR. *and* MRS. MOORE *help him with his heavy wraps*): I saw the lights so I came on in; the front door was unlocked.

MR. MOORE: Thank God you are here. Clarke is delirious —high fever.

MR. MOORE: And he's been talking out of his head—seeing

angels in the room—that's not normal. (CLARKE *stirs, sits up a bit*.)

PHYSICIAN (*taking his bag, getting thermometer, taking lad's temperature*): Quite high—infection somewhere—I hope it isn't that leg.

CLARKE: Am I getting any better? Will I be all right for Christmas?

PHYSICIAN: You'll be all right, sonny; you'll be all right. And don't worry about Christmas. Old Santa Claus can always find a way to visit every boy and girl—

CLARKE: I'm glad. Santa Claus will come to see me tonight. (*He closes his eyes*.)

PHYSICIAN (*after examination*): I'll have to put the cast on tomorrow. In the meantime, give him these pills regularly. He is a sick boy. (*Rising*): It's more than physical—he's heart sick.

MRS. MOORE: For the little pony?

PHYSICIAN: Possibly. But it's up to you, Mr. Moore, to make him want to get well—to give him something worth living for—

MR. MOORE: Isn't Christmas enough?

PHYSICIAN: If you make it attractive enough.

MR. MOORE (*puzzled; helping* PHYSICIAN *with coat and hat*): Attractive? Doctor, I'm a Hebrew professor, not an entertainer. How does one make Christmas more attractive than it is?

PHYSICIAN: I don't know, sir. No man knows what he can be or do until the time comes when he has to be or do something out of his line. But it is up to you to entertain the lad and to give him something that will take his mind off his pony—

MR. MOORE: I see. I'll do what I can, doctor; you know that. And we'll follow your orders to the letter.

PHYSICIAN: If he takes a turn for the worse, send for me; if I don't hear, I'll be back tomorrow morning. Goodnight, and a Merry Christmas to you both.

MR. *and* MRS. MOORE: Merry Christmas, Doctor; and many thanks for your help.

(*Exit* PHYSICIAN.)

51

MR. MOORE: Something to make him want to live—to take his mind off his little pony.

CLARKE (*opening his eyes, stirring*): Has Santa Claus come yet, daddy?

MR. MOORE (*at bedside*): Not yet, son.

CLARKE: Will I see him when he comes?

MRS. MOORE: Hardly, Clarke; you'll be fast asleep.

CLARKE: What will he look like?

MR. MOORE: Just like Santa Claus.

CLARKE: But what does Santa Claus look like? And how will he come?

MRS. MOORE (*to her husband*): Tell him, Clement. What does Santa Claus look like and how will he come? (*Doorbell rings; exit* MRS. MOORE.)

MR. MOORE (*turning up lamp, sitting by bedside*): Well, sonny, old Santa Claus will come tonight, when everything is hushed and still; when everything is so quiet around the house that—that—you can't even hear a mouse. After all the stockings have been hung by the fireplace—and all the children have gone fast asleep—

CLARKE (*becoming interested*): Will he come down the chimney?

MR. MOORE: If the house is locked up tight, that's the only way he can come, isn't it?

CLARKE: With a sleigh—all the way from the North Pole?

MR. MOORE: Yes, with a sleigh, and reindeer and presents for children, all the way from the North Pole.

(OFFSTAGE CHILDREN *sing "The First Noel"; one or two verses;* MR. MOORE *and* CLARKE *stop visiting and listen intently, until children go on down the street and voices fade away.*)

CLARKE: Are you going to put on your nightgown before he comes, daddy?

MR. MOORE: I'd better. If old Santa catches me with my suit on, he won't like it at all.

CLARKE: And will Santa look like old Mr. Jan at our Church?

MR. MOORE: Just like old Mr. Jan, the Dutchman. Short and fat; almost round; with a jolly face and dimpled cheeks and a big happy smile, and a lot of long white whiskers.

CLARKE (*sitting up, excitedly*): He will? Why, daddy, you never told me that before. Is there anything else you know about him?

MR. MOORE: Oh, there are lots of things about old Santa that you don't know.

CLARKE: Then tell me about them, daddy; and write them down so I can read about Santa to the children at school.

MR. MOORE: We can do better than that, Clarke; suppose we write a poem about it.

CLARKE: Good. A poem just for you and me—

MR. MOORE (*rising, going to the door*): And mummy.

CLARKE: All about Santa Claus coming on Christmas Eve. (*His eyes dance with joy*).

MR. MOORE (*calling out the door*): Catharine, bring a pencil and paper, please. Clarke and I have a job to do.

CLARKE: A big job, isn't it, daddy?

MR. MOORE: Why, yes, son; a man-sized job—

CLARKE: And a boy-sized job, too.

(*Enter* MRS. MOORE *with pencil and paper.*)

MRS. MOORE: The Greens called and sent their love. I can't imagine what you two are up to, but here's the paper and pencil. I'm going to look after the turkey while you men are at work.

(*Exit* MRS. MOORE.)

MR. MOORE (*as* CLARKE *sits up*): All ready, son?

CLARKE: Fluff up my pillows, daddy. (MR. MOORE *fluffs up the pillows, so lad is in a sitting position.*) That's better.

MR. MOORE (*sitting nearby, writing the lines as they form, reading them aloud as he writes them down.* ORGAN CHIMES *play, as if in far distance, familiar carols, such as: God Rest Ye Merry, Gentlemen; O Come All Ye Faithful; Away in a Manger; The First Noel; Gloria in Excelsis Deo; throughout the writing of the poem.*)

Twas the night before Christmas, and all through the house
Not a creature was stirring—

CLARKE: Not even a mouse.

MR. MOORE: Good; not even a mouse. What next?

CLARKE: The stockings.

MR. MOORE: Oh, yes.

The stockings were hung by the chimney with care

In hope that Saint Nicholas soon would be there.

CLARKE: The children were all fast asleep, remember?

MR. MOORE: Do I?

The children were nestled all snug in their beds

CLARKE: Dreaming of good things to eat—candy—cake—

MR. MOORE:

While visions of sugarplums danced in their heads.

CLARKE: While you and mummy were in your nightgowns, ready for bed.

MR. MOORE:

And Ma in her kerchief, and I in my cap

Had just settled down for a long winter's nap.

CLARKE: When Santa Claus woke you up—

MR. MOORE:

When out on the lawn there arose such a clatter

I sprang from my bed to see what was the matter.

Away to the window I flew in a flash,

Tore open the shutters and threw up the sash.

CLARKE: Was it snowing?

MR. MOORE: Yes; it had to be snowing.

The moon on the breast of the new-fallen snow

Gave the lustre of mid-day to objects below;

When what to my wondering eyes should appear

But a miniature sleigh and eight tiny reindeer.

CLARKE: Eight?

MR. MOORE: Four on each side; four pairs; just like a king or a queen, when they ride to be crowned.

CLARKE: Oh.

MR. MOORE:

With a little old driver so lively and quick

I knew in a moment, it must be— Who?

CLARKE: St. Nick.

MR. MOORE:

More rapid than eagles his coursers they came,

And he whistled and shouted and called them by name.

"Now Dasher, now Dancer, now Prancer and Vixen—

On Comet, On Cupid; On Donder and Blitzen—

To the top of the porch, to the top of the wall

Now dash away! dash away! dash away all!"

CLARKE: Were those the real names of the reindeer?

MR. MOORE: Can you think of any better names for reindeer? And if we name one of them Vixen, the name of the other would have to rhyme with it, so I made up Blitzen.

CLARKE: Goody; Vixen—Blitzen—that rhymes.

MR. MOORE: All right?

CLARKE: Yes; all right.

MR. MOORE: Now to really get poetic:
As dry leaves that before the wild hurricane fly,
When they meet with an obstacle, mount to the sky,
So up to the housetop his coursers they flew—

CLARKE: Daddy, what's a courser? That's the second time you've used that word and I don't get it.

MR. MOORE: A courser is a war horse, or a racer; one that is swift and spirited. I'm using it because Santa's reindeer will have to be swift and spirited if they're going to do all the work that is required of them on Christmas eve.

CLARKE: You're right there, daddy.

MR. MOORE:
So up to the housetop his coursers they flew
With a sleigh full of toys and St. Nicholas too.
And then, in a twinkling, I heard on the roof
The prancing and pawing of each little hoof.
As I drew in my head and was turning around
Down the chimney St. Nicholas came with a bound.

CLARKE: How was he dressed? Wasn't he covered with soot from the chimney?

MR. MOORE:
He was dressed all in fur, from his head to his foot,
And his clothes were all tarnished—

CLARKE: With ashes and soot.

MR. MOORE: Good.
A bundle of toys he had flung on his back
And he looked like a peddler just opening his pack.

CLARKE: Did he look like old Mr. Jan?

MR. MOORE: Yes, he did.
His eyes how they twinkled; his dimples how merry;
His cheeks were like roses; his nose like a—cherry!
His droll little mouth was drawn up like a bow

And the beard of his chin was white as—

CLARKE: The snow. And don't forget his pipe.

MR. MOORE:

The stump of a pipe he held tight in his teeth,
And the smoke it encircled his head like a wreath;
He had a broad face and little round stomach—

CLARKE: Stomach? What rhymes with stomach?

MR. MOORE: Nothing, I'm afraid; we'll have to change it.

He had a broad face and a little round belly,
That shook, when he laughed, like a bowl full of—

CLARKE: Jelly!

MR. MOORE:

He was chubby and plump; a right jolly old elf,
And I laughed when I saw him, in spite of myself.

Now what does he do?

CLARKE: He fills the stockings.

MR. MOORE: Of course he does.

A wink of his eye, and a twist of his head
Soon gave me to know I had nothing to dread;
He spoke not a word but went straight to his work,
And filled all the stockings; then turned with a jerk—

CLARKE: Don't forget old Mr. Jan—how he lays his finger
aside his nose—

MR. MOORE: We'll put that in right here.

And laying his finger aside of his nose,
And giving a nod, up the chimney he rose;
He sprang to his sleigh; to his team gave a whistle,
And away they all flew like the down of a thistle.

CLARKE: Didn't he wish everyone a Merry Christmas?

MR. MOORE: He certainly did.

But I heard him exclaim, ere he drove out of sight,
"Happy Christmas to all, and to all a goodnight."

CLARKE (calling): Mummy—Mummy—come in and see
what daddy and I did?

(Enter MRS. MOORE.)

MRS. MOORE: What did you do, Clarke?

CLARKE: We wrote a poem all about Santa Claus, and I'm
going to read it to the children in school after the holidays.
What are we going to name it, daddy?

Mr. Moore: We'll call it "A Visit from St. Nicholas."

Mrs. Moore (*standing by the bed*): Read it to me, please. I can hardly wait. It must be good medicine, because it's made our boy happy all over again.

Mr. Moore: Here it is. (*As he begins reading the first few lines,* Organ Chimes *grow louder, and then* Organ *plays first stanza "O Come All Ye Faithful"; as the music swells and reader's voice fades, Curtain closes on the scene.*)

Narrator: Dr. Clement Clarke Moore had no idea of writing a famous poem that Christmas Eve in 1822. In fact he was a bit critical of what he called "frivolous amusements," and deplored the fact that "more of the well-disposed among my young countrymen do not devote their leisure hours to the attainment of useful learning." However, a friend of the Moores, the daughter of Rev. David Butler of Troy, New York, visiting in their New York City home that same Christmas season, discovered the poem and copied it into her personal album. Unknown to the author, she sent a copy to the editor of her hometown newspaper, The Troy Sentinel. He published it the following year in the issue of December 23, 1823, under the heading, "Account of a visit from St. Nicholas or Santa Claus"; and he added this explanatory note, "We know not to whom we are indebted for the description of that unwearied patron of children, but from whomever it may have come, we give thanks for it." Dr. Moore was a bit chagrined when he learned that his verses had appeared in print, deeming it beneath the dignity of a professor of Hebrew in a Theological Seminary. But the response of the public was immediate and enthusiastic. The dignified professor finally acknowledged his authorship in a volume of his original poems published twenty-two years later, in 1844, which included this now-universal favorite.

The year following the writing of these lines, 1823, the Diocesan Seminary merged with the General Theological Seminary, and Dr. Moore became Professor of Oriental Literature, a post he occupied until his resignation in 1850. He produced a monumental work entitled: "A Compendious Lexicon of the Hebrew Language: In Two Volumes," but children the world over remember him for that bit of frivolous verse he wrote for his little boy one Christmas Eve years ago. He passed away on July 10, 1863, his eighty-fourth year, and is buried in Trinity Cemetery, Broadway and 155th Street, New York City. Each Christmas Eve, children come to his grave, carrying lighted lanterns, and singing carols, honoring the minister-professor who gave Santa Claus to Christmas.

(*Exit* NARRATOR.)

CHRISTMAS TRADITIONS

A PLAY
in
ONE ACT

CHRISTMAS TRADITIONS

3 men
3 women

CHARACTERS

MR. AND MRS. JACKSON; typical middle-aged American couple.
Their four teen age children: Ted, Sara, Jack, Jane.
SETTING: A typical living room in a middle-class American home, on
  Christmas Eve. The room has comfortable chairs, sofa, small end
  table, lamps, magazine racks, book cases, piano, fireplace and
  mantle in center against back stage wall. Space in mid-center is
  cleared for the Christmas tree. Windows, for holly wreaths, and
  other period furniture complete the warm, friendly, inviting
  atmosphere of the room.
TIME: Christmas Eve.
MATERIALS: A large Christmas tree and stand; strings of tree lights;
  assorted candles; holly, mistletoe, Christmas cards; packages and
  wrapping paper, stickers, tape, cord; miscellaneous tree decorations;
  magazines, newspapers.

(*Curtain is raised on the scene described above. After a few
moments,* MR. *and* MRS. JACKSON *enter, laden down with
Christmas bundles and packages. They are followed by the two
girls,* SARA *and* JANE, *who carry the tree decorations; bringing
up the rear come the boys,* TED *and* JACK, *carrying the large
Christmas tree. The scene is one of gaiety, excitement and
activity. Just as he enters,* MR. JACKSON *turns, calls through
the door.*)

MR. JACKSON: Hurry up with the tree, boys.

TED (*offstage*): We're coming, Dad. Just a minute.

JACK: This thing is heavy.

(TED *and* JACK *bring in the tree, as the girls put their decorations down on the floor in the center of the room.* MRS. JACK-
SON *goes to the table with her bundles and begins slowly, carefully wrapping packages. She continues this during the entire
scene; wrapping, decorating and addressing packages.* MR.

Jackson *places his bundles down on the sofa. The boys set up the tree in the middle of the room, and all the children begin decorating it. The girls continue with this; but, after a while,* Ted *goes over to help his mother with the packages, sitting behind the table as he works. As soon as she finishes hanging some decorations,* Sara *exits and re-enters shortly with some holly; sitting near the foot of the sofa she begins making a holly wreath.* Mr. Jackson *helps with some of the decorating.*)

Mr. Jackson (*to* Jane, *who is sorting through the decorations*): Jane, bring some of that tinsel over on this side of the tree.

Jane: All right, Dad. (*She does so.*) Is that better?

Mr. Jackson: Much better, dear. (Jack *begins hanging up, straightening out, the strings of lights for the tree, working them until they are hung properly, and lighted.*)

Mrs. Jackson (*to* Ted): How is your package wrapping coming, Ted?

Ted (*coldly*): I guess it's O.K., Mom. But I was never cut out for this fancy wrapping and stickers and stuff. I reckon there are some kids who don't even have presents to give, so maybe I'm pretty lucky after all.

Mrs. Jackson: That's right, Teddy; just suppose there were no presents to give? Think how empty Christmas would be.

Jack (*working on the lights*): Dad, have we been decorating Christmas trees ever since we were kids?

Mr. Jackson (*continuing with the decorating*): Almost that long, son. You see, when you were a baby, you either went to bed early or sat in your crib and looked on. But mother and I have been doing this every year since we were married.

Jack: And did your folks have a tree each Christmas too?

Mr. Jackson: Of course, son. Trees and Christmas go together—

Ted: Like ham and eggs—

Jane: Or like cream and sugar—

Mr. Jackson: Well, they do go together. Without a tree, Christmas wouldn't really seem like Christmas. I don't know whether the holiday season would be pleasant without a gaily decorated Christmas tree.

JACK: Have people been celebrating Christmas with trees ever since Jesus was born?

MR. JACKSON: Not exactly that long. No one really knows when the first tree was used. Some give Saint Boniface the credit.

SARA: Who was he, Dad?

MR. JACKSON: One of the saints that we call one of the early Church Fathers. He was a missionary to Germany during the eighth century. He encouraged the decorating of a fir tree inside the house to counteract the pagan custom of sacrificing human beings to what they called a sacred oak tree.

MRS. JACKSON: Is that a true story?

MR. JACKSON: I wouldn't vouch for it; but it is one of the legends that has been handed down for untold generations, just like many other traditions associated with Christmas. But the truth is that trees and lights and gifts and decorations came into existence long after Jesus was born.

TED: Tell us about it, Dad.

MR. JACKSON: About the first Christmas tree?

TED: Yes; tell us about it.

MR. JACKSON: If you promise to keep on with your work, I'll try.

SARA (*solemnly*): We promise.

MR. JACKSON (*sitting on the sofa, as the others continue with their Christmas Eve chores*): There are many stories about the first tree. But let me ask a question first. Who was Joseph of Arimathaea?

SARA: I know; he was the rich man who gave his tomb in the garden for Jesus' burial. Is that right?

MR. JACKSON: Yes, Sara; that is right.

JACK: He was one of the secret disciples, like Nicodemus, wasn't he, Dad?

MR. JACKSON: I think so, Jack. Several who did not follow Jesus openly before his death, but stood up for him after the resurrection, are called "secret disciples" and I believe Joseph was one of these.

TED: But what has that got to do with a Christmas tree?

MR. JACKSON: Well, Ted, the story goes that after Jesus' ascension, Joseph did become an open and avowed follower of the Christian Way. Not only that, we are told that he even became a missionary, and travelled as far as the British Isles.

TED: On foot?

MR. JACKSON: More than likely. There wasn't any other method of transportation for poor people.

TED: I thought you said he was a rich man?

MRS. JACKSON: Ted, when he became a Christian he must have given his fortune away like another rich man, Barnabas, did about the same time.

TED: Oh. But if he walked all that distance, he must have been *some* missionary. Then what, Dad?

MR. JACKSON: When he arrived at a place called Wyrral-hill, he stuck his staff into the ground, and it supposedly took root and grew into a lovely evergreen tree. So, we are told, the English people began cutting down trees and decorating them at Christmas time in commemoration of the travels of this devout and worthy man.

JACK: Sounds rather strange, doesn't it?

SARA: It sure does, Jack. Why would people want to cut down trees commemorating the life of a man who was supposed to have planted one? It doesn't make sense to me.

MR. JACKSON: Nor to me, Sara. One never knows how these stories begin or how they are altered with the years. But there is an even more beautiful and fanciful story that comes from Germany, if you want to hear it.

TED: Fire away; it can't be any more impossible than that one about Joseph.

MRS. JACKSON: I'm afraid you children will become so interested in these legends that you will neglect your work.

JANE: We're listening and working at the same time, Mother.

MRS. JACKSON: All right, dear. Just don't become *too* wrapped up in what Daddy is saying.

MR. JACKSON: This story is about as true as the other one. Hundreds of years ago Christmas came quietly and uneventfully to the lonely home of a hard-working German woodcutter. Outside, the wind was blowing fiercely through the branches of the trees. Inside, about a happy fire, the family gathered to hear again the age-old story of the birth of Jesus. Just as they were about to retire, there was a sudden and surprising knock at the door. The father opened the door and, to his surprise, saw a young lad, cold and shivering. They welcomed him in gladly, gave him food and something hot to drink. The wood-cutter's son, Hans, even offered the stranger his own bed in which to sleep.

JACK: That's more than Ted would do.

TED: You have room to talk, big boy.

MRS. JACKSON: Boys, please; let Daddy finish.

MR. JACKSON: Very early the next morning, Christmas Day, they were awakened by music from a heavenly choir. To their astonishment, they discovered that their visitor was the Christ child. As he left the cottage, he took a twig from a fir tree, and planted it in the ground. And, to the family that had welcomed him, he said, "I have gladly received your gifts, and here is mine for you; this tree will never fail to bear its fruit, and you shall always have abundance."

JANE: A lovely story, Dad, but could such an impossible legend have started the widespread use of trees throughout the Christian world?

MR. JACKSON: Hardly, Jane. Even the tradition that on the night of his birth, all the trees of the forest bloomed and bore fruit, would not account for our modern custom.

TED: Is that all there is to it? Just some absurd legends?

MR. JACKSON: No, Teddy. If we discard all of these stories, and look for the real origin of the Christmas tree custom, we find it in Germany, in the home of the great Protestant reformer, Martin Luther.

JANE: The same Luther who wrote "Away in a Manger" and "A Mighty Fortress is our God"?

MR. JACKSON: Yes, Jane, the very same Martin Luther. The man who wrote the first Christmas lullaby also introduced the first Christmas tree.

JACK: When was that?

MR. JACKSON: About the year 1535. Luther became entranced with the wonder and beauty of the starry skies on a clear Christmas Eve, and naturally his thoughts turned to Jesus who had come from above for our salvation; returning home, he set up an evergreen tree for his children, and placed lighted candles on the branches and a large candle at the top. When his children asked him about it, he replied, 'This tree represents the dark night of our Saviour's birth. The small candles represent the stars that twinkled in a deep sea of blue, and the large taper on top is for the Star of Bethlehem, which hung over the place where the infant lay.'

TED: Then a white tree isn't really a Christian Christmas tree, is it?

MR. JACKSON: I don't think it could be, son. White trees must have come many years later, for people who wanted to enjoy a tree at Christmas without having one that had a definite Christian significance.

JANE: A Christmas tree without Christ.

MR. JACKSON: That's right, Jane. A Christmas tree without Christ.

SARA: How did the custom spread from Germany to the United States?

MR. JACKSON: Many years after Luther put up his tree—in 1840, if my memory is correct, a large tree was set up in Paris. It took those centuries for the custom to spread from one nation to its nearest neighbour.

JACK: I wouldn't say that Germany and France are neighbours. From what I read of history, they are perpetual enemies. Maybe that's why it took so long.

MR. JACKSON: You may be right, Jack. I never thought of it that way. But the very next year, 1841, Queen Victoria set up a large beautifully decorated tree in Windsor Castle, and its future in England was assured.

JACK: Do Christians all over the world use trees?

MR. JACKSON: Practically all; at least in every land where evergreen trees are available. The tree also represents Christ, the tree of life.

JANE: And the lights, the candles on the branches—

MR. JACKSON: Christ, the light of the world.

(MR. JACKSON *sits back, picks up a magazine and begins to read;* JACK *plugs in the Christmas tree lights. Exit* JANE, *to re-enter with a box of large candles. She sits on the floor near* SARA, *who is at work on a holly wreath.*)

JANE: Mother, will these candles be all right? I thought we could place them in the windows and light them later on to-night.

MRS. JACKSON: That will be fine, dear. I'll help you when I finish with these packages. Just arrange them as you think best if I'm not through here when you're ready.

SARA: And I'll put a holly wreath around each one. Will that be all right?

JANE: Of course. (*To her father*): Daddy, what about candles and lights in the windows on Christmas Eve? Where did that custom originate?

MR. JACKSON (*putting down his magazine*): Just a minute! I'm not a walking encyclopedia. Am I expected to remember everything I ever read or heard? Now what was that, Jane?

JANE: I was wondering where lighted candles came from and where they were first used and why they are associated with this season of the year.

MR. JACKSON: Jane, that custom antedates the tree. Of course, the legends that have grown up with the centuries try to connect every custom with Jesus himself. Some say he wanders all over the world again each Christmas Eve, bearing great bundles of evergreens on his back. Through busy city streets, down dark deserted alleys, up and down bleak country roads and lanes he wanders, to the proudest mansion and the lowliest hovel, to be welcomed or rejected as he goes from house to house.

SARA: Frightening thought, isn't it?

MR. JACKSON: It is. In Ireland, devout Christians placed lighted candles in their windows to light the Christ-child's way, and to tell him that here was warmth, food, shelter, clothing and companionship. And then in other places, Christ is supposed to come as a beggar seeking alms at a lighted window, and benevolence shown to the beggars was looked upon as hospitality to Christ. But the candle is symbolic of Christ, the light of the world, turning night into day, radiating warmth as well as light wherever He goes.

JANE: So every little thing connected with Christmas is symbolic of some Christian truth.

MR. JACKSON: Exactly. The customs which the Church could not discard it consecrated, made symbolic of some holy message. So today we enjoy the customs and traditions of many lands, all made holy through Christian consecration.

(JANE *rises, places her candles in the window (or atop the mantle), lights them.* SARA *places a holly wreath about each, and they stand back to watch.*)

SARA: Now that that is finished, I have a question for Dad.

MR. JACKSON: What is it this time, Sara?

SARA (*sitting on the sofa*): You told Jack and Ted about the tree, and Jane about the lights. I want you to tell me about the holly. When was it used, and why do we have it at Christmas?

MR. JACKSON (*as* JANE *helps the boys decorate the tree*): Suppose we take your questions one at a time, Sara. Now which one was first?

SARA: Why do we use holly as a decoration?

MR. JACKSON: Holly used to be a symbol of marriage.

SARA: Marriage?

MR. JACKSON: Yes. It was supposed to represent the dark monotony of marriage and the many thorns which abound.

TED: Dad, you have spoken a parable.

SARA: Ted, its my turn; you hush. Go on, Daddy; tell me about the holly.

MR. JACKSON: There's an old carol called "The holly and the ivy." Holly was the man's plant and ivy the woman's. But its real connection with Christmas lies in the fact that it connects the two great festivals of the Christian year, Christmas and Easter. It reminds us that the babe we all adore at Christmas grew up to be the man whom the world "despised and rejected." When they slew him on Good Friday, they placed a crown of thorns on his brow, which drew great drops of blood. And holly is symbolic of that crown of thorns and the red berries stand for the great drops of blood. So at Christmas the mystery of his birth and the mystery of his death are linked together, as they were during the Middle Ages.

JANE: Daddy, while we are talking about plants and decorations, would you mind telling us about the mistletoe?

(SARA *browses through a magazine.*)

TED: Huh! Just like a girl; always thinking about boys and kissing games.

JACK: Post office, here I come!

MRS. JACKSON: Teddy, please; don't be rude.

TED: Well ask her what she did with that piece of mistletoe I saw her buy downtown the other day?

JANE (*angrily*): Mother; make him behave! After all, it's none of his business.

MR. JACKSON: Now where does that get us? Jane has the mistletoe and Ted has to behave.

JANE: Let's start all over again. I wanted to know what mistletoe had to do with Christmas.

MR. JACKSON: The ancient Britons had a custom centuries ago whereby the annual cutting of the mistletoe was quite an important event.

JACK: I don't doubt that a bit!

MR. JACKSON: You're ahead of my story, Jack. Kissing wasn't associated with mistletoe at that time.

JACK: Oh, that's different.

MR. JACKSON: As I was saying, before the family Romeo interrupted, this ceremony took place in November of each year. The people marched in stately procession to one of the selected trees, led by the tribal priest. The priest then would climb the tree, cut off the sprigs of mistletoe and let them fall. They were caught in a large cloth held outstretched for that purpose by the lovely girls of the tribe.

JACK: Lovely girls? Here's where I came in!

MR. JACKSON: Jack, please; let me finish my story.

JACK: All right.

MR. JACKSON: The precious sprigs were carried to each home and hung over the doors to ward off evil spirits and bring good health to all in the house.

TED: Like we hang up horse-shoes and carry a rabbit's foot?

MR. JACKSON: It served about the same purpose.

TED: But she wants to know where the kissing part came in.

MRS. JACKSON: Teddy, that's enough; no more of this teasing, boys; please.

MR. JACKSON: Just where that came in is a mystery. It may have come in this manner. If a man had a grievance against his neighbour and wished to forgive him, he would have the priest place a bit of mistletoe over his door; and if the neighbour saw it and was willing to do the forgiving or receive forgiveness, he would have the priest place a sprig over *his* door. And what would be more natural than that the two erring neighbours, seeing each other's mistletoe, would meet in the street between their two houses, give each other the embrace of forgiveness and in the emotion of the moment, bestow upon each other the kiss of forgiveness?

Mrs. Jackson: And the boys and girls, peeking through the living room windows, said one to another, "This thing has infinite possibilities."

Mr. Jackson (as all laugh): True enough, Mother, true enough. From the street it spread to the front porch, and then into the hall and back in the dining room and even to the kitchen. I don't know whether that retreat can be called progress or not!

Jack: That reminds me of the girl in school who nicknamed her best beau Pilgrim, because every time he came around he made a little progress!

Ted: At least that's one case where you advance backwards or retreat forwards. But Dad, I believe it's my time for a question, isn't it?

Mr. Jackson: I believe so, Teddy. What is it?

Ted: Mom always cooks mince pies during Christmas. Is there any special reason why we have them at this season? Couldn't we have mince pies just as well for Easter or the Fourth of July?

Sara: Disgusting—disgusting—always thinking of your stomach.

Jane: Just like a boy, Sara. Always thinking of stuffing himself.

Mr. Jackson: Now, girls, take it easy. Ted happens to be right this time.

Ted: For once in my life, and I hope all of you take notice.

Mr. Jackson: Mince pies do have a connection with Christmas. But let me ask a question. What were the gifts of the wise men?

Sara: Gold, frankincense and myrrh.

Mr. Jackson: Right; now where did the wise men come from?

Ted: The east.

Mr. Jackson: Correct; and since poor folks have neither gold nor frankincense nor myrrh, we go to the east for our spices, and we take those same spices and make from them or with them a mincemeat, with which we make the pie.

JACK: And remember the Magi at Christmas dinner?

MR. JACKSON: Yes, Jack; in eating mincemeat pies, we remember the gifts of the wise men. People have been doing that since about the year 1600.

TED: Daddy, isn't frankincense just ancient Air-wick?

MR. JACKSON (*as the others laugh*): What? Air-wick? What do you mean, Ted?

TED: I figured out that frankincense was burned before a king; and since in olden times people didn't take baths or wash their clothes, and the animals lived in the houses and castles with the people, those places must have smelled pretty bad.

JACK: I don't doubt that a bit.

MR. JACKSON: Go on.

TED: So the king would burn frankincense to kill all the other odors. It was just an expensive incense that only kings could afford. Poor people either had to burn a cheap incense or do without.

MR. JACKSON: Son, you may have solved a mystery there. I knew frankincense was burned for or before a king, but I never figured out why. You may have stumbled on a solution.

MRS. JACKSON: And in that connection, there's enough hot water so everyone can take a bath before going to bed tonight —including the two young gentlemen of the house.

JACK: And I figured out all about the Yule log, Dad.

MR. JACKSON: How's that, Jack?

JACK: People are always getting sentimental about the bringing in of the Yule log every Christmas. I figured out that most of those poor folks went out and cut down some wood for their fires every day; when the holidays came they wanted to rest and relax and play and enjoy themselves, so a group of them went out and cut down some large trees and dragged in enough large logs to burn for the whole week.

MR. JACKSON: You mean they were just too lazy to do that the rest of the year?

JACK: Something like that. It's reasonable, isn't it? As reasonable as Ted and his Air-wick?

MR. JACKSON: I'd give you both the same credit, I'll have to admit.

(*Exit* JANE.)

71

MRS. JACKSON (*calling out the door*): Jane, do you have all the Christmas cards? We want them in here so we can look over them again tomorrow.

JANE (*offstage*): I have them, mother; I'll bring them in in a minute.

(*Exit SARA, returning with tray, cups, saucers, cookies, hot chocolate, which she serves to all the family. Enter JANE with pile of cards which she places on the table. She sits beside TED at the table and they look through the cards.*)

JANE: Dad, what about Christmas cards?

TED: I think they are a lot of bother.

MR. JACKSON: You may be surprised to know that this is about the only real English contribution to Christmas. The first card was made by an Englishman, J. C. Horsley, a member of the Royal Academy, in 1845. It had a family picture on it, featuring three generations of the family circle; there were two smaller pictures showing hungry people being fed and thinly clad children being clothed. And the family was saying what we have been saying ever since, "A Merry Christmas and a Happy New Year to You."

MRS. JACKSON: And we have never improved on those words.

JACK: If that is the only English contribution to Christmas, what have Americans given?

MR. JACKSON: Pathetically enough, only turkey and cranberry sauce. But going back to cards, the year after that first card was sent, the year 1846, about a thousand were exchanged in England. Since then cards of all shapes, sizes and descriptions have flooded the market and millions are exchanged every year.

SARA: One more thing, Dad, before we stop. Where did Santa Claus come from?

MRS. JACKSON: That reminds me, I forgot to hang up my stocking!

MR. JACKSON: All joking aside, there was a real man named St. Nicholas. We call him Santa Claus, but some others call him St. Nick, or Kris Kringle. But the original Nicholas was a bishop of the church, stationed at Myra, in Asia Minor.

SARA: Did he have a fat tummy and a red suit and jingle bells?

MR. JACKSON: I don't know, Sara. You see, he was quite a wealthy man, even though a Christian leader. In fact, he was reported to have been so wealthy that he carried with him a symbol of his wealth wherever he went: either three purses filled with money for charitable purposes, or else three gold balls.

JACK: Three gold balls? Why, that's the sign of the pawn shops!

MR. JACKSON: You ought to know, son. By the way, whatever happened to that watch we gave you for graduation? You remember it, don't you?

JACK: If it's all the same to you, we won't go into that right now.

MR. JACKSON: Fair enough. The symbol of Bishop Nicholas' wealth and giving later came to represent those who gave money and alms; and still later, those who loaned money instead. Formerly, at the sign of three gold balls, the poor could find free food, clothing and shelter; the slave could be ransomed and the helpless find succor.

TED: I always heard that the three gold balls meant "Two to one you never get it back."

JANE: And that bishop was really the first Santa Claus?

MR. JACKSON: Yes, Jane. One night he is said to have flipped a gold coin up in the air, aiming at a chimney top of a poor widow's cottage. The widow's son had gotten his feet wet and his shoes were drying before the open fire. With accurate aim, the bishop's coin hit the bull's eye, fell down the chimney and bounced into the lad's shoe. He found it there the next day.

TED: And the following Christmas Eve he remembered it.

MR. JACKSON: Yes.

JACK: And his mother didn't want to disappoint him so she filled it with good things to eat as a surprise.

SARA: And some smarty decided that his mother's stocking would hold a lot more than his own shoe—and we've been hanging up stockings ever since. Is that right?

MR. JACKSON: Not bad, Sara. That little boy who got his feet wet started something that has become universally part of Christmas. And all gifts are given in honor of that St. Nicholas.

TED: That reminds me of a story some fellow told in Sunday

73

School. We were arguing about the devil, and he said he didn't believe in the devil, because the devil was just like Santa Claus. It was your father all the time!

MRS. JACKSON: Now, Ted, you could have left that unsaid.

TED: I was only telling what one of the fellows said. It wasn't my idea.

SARA: I hope not!

MR. JACKSON: Have we covered everything?

JANE (*looking up from her cards*): Just about, Dad. All except the Christmas bells.

"I heard the bells on Christmas day
Their old familiar carols play,
And wild and sweet the words repeat
Of peace on earth, good will to men."

SARA: I know one about the bells, too.

"Ring out, wild bells, to the wild wild sky,
The flying cloud, the frosty light;
The year is dying in the night;
Ring out, wild bells, and let him die."

MR. JACKSON: Any more poets?

TED: I'll risk it. (*He sings a chorus of "Jingle Bells" and all applaud.*)

MRS. JACKSON: And where did the bells come from? What do they mean?

MR. JACKSON: Bells were rung on two occasions, other than to summon worshippers to services. They were tolled for a death, and rung joyously for a birth. So we ring the bells to herald the birth of Christ, and the death of Satan and the powers of sin and darkness.

MRS. JACKSON: And why do we celebrate Christmas on December 25? Surely if Jesus had been born in the middle of winter, the shepherds would not have been out on the hills "keeping watch over their flocks by night." They would have been in the warm shelter of the fold.

SARA: And the people wouldn't have been able to make the trips back to their birthplaces if the roads had been covered with ice and snow.

JANE: Surely Joseph wouldn't have taken Mary on such a dangerous journey, in view of the imminent birth of her baby.

MR. JACKSON: All that you say is true. The Bible gives no definite date. No one knows the exact time of Jesus' birth. But the great Councils of early Christendom agreed on the date of December 25 because of its symbolic significance.

MRS. JACKSON: What do you mean by that?

MR. JACKSON: The longest day of the year is June 21. After that day, the days begin to grow smaller, shorter, and the nights begin to swallow up the days, second by second, minute by minute, until we come to December 21 or 22, which is the shortest day of the year. Then the days once again begin to encroach upon the night; the days begin to swallow up the darkness of the nights. So these leaders decided upon December 25, as the one date when, for a certainty, the days begin to destroy and swallow up the nights. It is symbolic of Him who came as the light of the world to destroy all of the powers of darkness.

MRS. JACKSON: "The light shineth in the darkness, and the darkness comprehendeth it not." The darkness could not, cannot, put it out.

JANE: And what about the carols, Daddy?

MR. JACKSON: Really, children, it is getting late, and tomorrow will be a very busy day. The tree is finished, isn't it, Jack?

JACK: Yes, Dad; all finished.

JANE: Then suppose we all sing a verse or two of "Silent Night" as we straighten up the room. (*She goes to the piano, strikes a chord, and all sing as they straighten up the room together. If no piano is available, they sing unaccompanied. As they sing the last line of the last stanza, they slowly exit one by one with* MR. JACKSON *bringing up the rear. As the singing ceases,* MR. JACKSON *turns, and speaks to the assembled audience.*)

MR. JACKSON (*at the door*): Good night, folks, and a Merry Christmas and a Happy New Year to you all. Good night.

(*Exit* MR. JACKSON.)

CURTAIN

Note: The effect of the play will be found in its simplicity and naturalness, with the preparations for Christmas going along smoothly and carefully. If the parts for MR. JACKSON are too long and difficult for memorizing, sheets of paper containing the script of the play may be pasted in the pages of a magazine. Thus he may at his leisure browse through the magazine during lulls in the play, and pick up the stories and speeches as they come due, relieving him of the necessity of a great deal of memorizing. This is suggested since it has been done effectively on several occasions in the past.

THE RESURRECTION

AN EASTER PAGEANT
by
Ernest K. Emurian

Playing Time: About forty minutes.

THE RESURRECTION*

An Easter Pageant

by

Ernest K. Emurian

Cast: 15 men, older boys; 3 women, or older girls; Musician; Singers.

CHARACTERS

Narrator (a Minister if possible)
Organist or Pianist
Choir, or Soloist, Quartet etc.
Joseph of Arimathaea
Nicodemus
Two Male Servants
Three Women: (Mary, mother of Jesus; Mary of Magdala; Salome)
Two Roman Guards (tall men)
Two Male Angels (Inside and Outside angels)
Peter (older)
John (younger)
Two Priests
Cleopas and Companion (two followers, men)

All characters garbed in dress typical of their position and for this particular period of history.
Setting: The tomb in Joseph's garden. Tomb is center of stage; may be constructed out of plywood, masonite, or merely with a board frame, covered with cheesecloth material; frontpiece may be all that is necessary, with sides and top covered with material. Large flat round stone-like piece for door, placed over opening in front of tomb. Inside Angel in tomb before the pageant begins; also in tomb is large brilliant spotlight, ready to be cut on or plugged in at moment's notice; palms, lilies, a bench or two, complete the setting.
Time: The first Easter.

Note: This play is included by permission of THE PROGRESSIVE FARMER, Birmingham, Ala.

(Lights dimmed; Musician plays hymn "Beneath the Cross of Jesus," setting stage and atmosphere for pageant.)

NARRATOR reads: The Agony in the Garden; Matt. 26: 36-46.

"Then cometh Jesus with the disciples unto a place called Gethsemane, and saith unto them, Sit ye here while I go yonder and pray; and he took Peter and James and John and began to be sorrowful and very heavy; then he saith to them, My soul is exceeding sorrowful even unto death; tarry ye here and watch with me. And he went a little further and fell on his face and prayed, saying, O my father, if it be possible, let this cup pass from me; nevertheless not as I will but as thou wilt. And he cometh unto the disciples and findeth them asleep, and saith unto Peter, What, could ye not watch with me one hour? Watch and pray that ye enter not into temptation; the spirit indeed is willing but the flesh is weak. He went again the second time and prayed, O my father, if this cup may not pass away from me except I drink it, thy will be done. And he came and found them asleep again, for their eyes were heavy; and he left them and went away again and prayed the third time, saying the same words. Then cometh he to his disciples and saith unto them, Sleep on now and take your rest; behold, the hour is at hand, and the son of man is betrayed into the hands of sinners; rise, let us be going; behold he that betrayeth me is at hand."

CHOIR: Hymn "Into the Woods My Master Went" (Lutkin); both stanzas.

NARRATOR reads: The Arrest and Crucifixion. John 19:1-3; 14-16.

"Then Pilate therefore took Jesus and scourged him and the soldiers plaited a crown of thorns and put it on his head, and they put a purple robe on him and said, Hail, King of the Jews! And they smote him with their hands."

"And it was the preparation of the Passover, and about the sixth hour, and he said unto the Jews, Behold your King. But they cried out, Away with him; away with him, crucify him. Pilate saith unto them, Shall I crucify your King? The chief priests answered, We have no King but Caesar. Then delivered he him therefore unto them to be crucified, and they took Jesus and led him away."

(*Shadow of cross appears in front of church, projected from lantern in rear; or else a robed youth appears quietly in front, carrying large pasteboard cross, which he holds aloft during the reading.*)

Matt. 27:33-38.

"And when they were come to a place called Golgotha, that is to say, a place of a skull, they gave him vinegar to drink mingled with gall; and when he had tasted thereof he would not drink it; and they crucified him, and parted his garments, casting lots, that it might be fulfilled which was spoken by the prophets: They parted my garments among them and upon my vesture did they cast lots. And sitting down they watched him there, and set up over his head his accusation, written, This is Jesus, the King of the Jews. Then were there two thieves crucified with him, one on the right hand and the other on the left."

CHOIR: Hymn "When I Survey the Wondrous Cross" (Tune: Hamburg; Stanzas one and three.)

Narrator continues:

Luke 23:39-46.

"And one of the malefactors that were hanged railed on him, saying, If thou be Christ, save thyself and us; but the other answering rebuked him, saying, Dost thou not fear God, seeing thou art in the same condemnation? And we indeed justly, for we receive the due reward of our deeds; but this man hath done nothing amiss. And he said unto Jesus, Lord, remember me when thou comest into thy kingdom. And Jesus said unto him, Verily I say unto thee, Today shalt thou be with me in Paradise. And it was about twelve o'clock noon; and there was darkness over all the earth until three o'clock; and the sun was darkened and the veil of the temple was rent in the midst; and when Jesus had cried with a loud voice, he said, Father, into thy hands I commend my spirit. And having said thus, he gave up the ghost."

CHOIR: Spiritual, "Were You There When They Crucified My

Lord." (Two stanzas; for second stanza use: "Were You There When They Nailed Him to the Tree.")

(*Exit robed youth with cross; or cut off shadow of cross projected from rear; as cross fades, soft blue light covers stage, quite dim.*)

Enter

JOSEPH, NICODEMUS, TWO MALE SERVANTS, bearing stretcher— with pillows covered with sheet to resemble a body—followed at distance by the TWO MARYS; they roll stone away; servants place body in tomb; roll stone back in place; stand watching.

NARRATOR: John 19:38-42

"And after this, Joseph of Arimathaea, being a disciple of Jesus, but secretly for fear of the Jews, besought Pilate that he might take away the body of Jesus; and Pilate gave him leave. He came therefore and took the body of Jesus, and there came also Nicodemus, who at the first came to Jesus by night, and brought a mixture of myrrh and aloes about a hundred pound weight. Then took they the body of Jesus and wound it in linen cloths with the spices as the manner of the Jews is to bury.

Now in the place where he was crucified there was a garden and in the garden a new sepulcher, wherein was never yet man laid. There laid they Jesus, therefore, because of the Jews preparation day. For the sepulcher was nigh at hand."

Matt. 27:61

"And there was Mary Magdalene and the other Mary sitting over against the sepulcher."

CHOIR: "In Joseph's Lovely Garden" (Dickinson) (First stanza).

(Exit entire Burial Party as Musician plays above anthem tune once more.)

Enter
Two Roman Guards, with uniform, helmets, spears, sandals; seal tomb, stand watch at either side of the stone.

NARRATOR: Matt. 27:62-66

"Now the next day that followed the day of preparation, the chief priests and Pharisees came together unto Pilate saying, Sir, we remember that this deceiver said while he was yet alive, After three days I will rise again. Command therefore that the sepulcher be made sure until the third day, lest his disciples come by night and steal him away, and say unto the people, He is risen from the dead; so the last error be worse than the first. Pilate said unto them, Ye have a watch; Go your way; make it sure, as sure as you can. So they went, and made the sepulcher sure, sealing the stone and setting a watch."

CHOIR: Hymn "Low in the Grave He Lay" (Christ Arose) (Lowry) (*Use first stanza very softly; no chorus. Use second stanza, softly, followed immediately by full voice* CHORUS, *"Up from the grave He arose" etc.*)

(*As* CHOIR *sings chorus, flash bulbs from several cameras about and inside tomb flash brilliantly;* INSIDE ANGEL *plugs in, or cuts on, strong spotlight inside tomb;* TWO ROMAN GUARDS, *seeing flashes of light, look about in amazed surprise, then fall to their faces in front of tomb and lie there prostrate.* OUTSIDE ANGEL *enters, and, with help of* INSIDE ANGEL, *rolls stone away from door, to one side.* TWO ANGELS *stand, one just inside, one outside tomb. (All this takes place very suddenly, dramatically, while* CHOIR *is singing chorus to second stanza of above hymn.) At end of chorus,* TWO ROMAN GUARDS *get up excitedly, and flee from the stage in terror, running through the entire length of the building to the rear.*)

CHOIR: "Low in the Grave He Lay" (third stanza and chorus; full voice).

(*Exit* OUTSIDE ANGEL *to one side.*)

Enter

THREE WOMEN (Two Marys and Salome); they act out in pantomime this story as it is being read. INSIDE ANGEL gestures as he too acts out his part.

NARRATOR: Mark 16:1-7

"And when the Sabbath was past, Mary Magdalene and Mary the mother of Jesus, and Salome had bought sweet spices that they might come and anoint him. And very early in the morning the first day of the week, they came unto the sepulcher at the rising of the sun. And they said among themselves, Who shall roll us away the stone from the door of the sepulcher? And when they looked, they saw that the stone was rolled away, for it was very great. And entering into the sepulcher they saw a young man sitting on the right side, clothed in a long white garment; and they were afraid; And he saith unto them: Be not affrighted. Ye seek Jesus of Nazareth who was crucified. He is not here; behold the place where they laid him. But go your way; tell his disciples and Peter that he goeth before you into Galilee; there shall ye see him as he said unto you."

CHOIR: "In Joseph's Lovely Garden" (Dickinson) (Second stanza; as WOMEN peer into and about open tomb; INSIDE ANGEL sits in view just inside door pointing to place where Jesus lay).

Exit

THREE WOMEN hurriedly.

NARRATOR: Mark 16:8

"And they went out quickly and fled from the sepulcher for they

84

trembled and were amazed; neither said they anything to any man for they were afraid."

Exit
INSIDE ANGEL to one side.

MUSICIAN plays music "In Joseph's Lovely Garden" once.

Enter
MARY MAGDALENE from rear; followed by PETER and JOHN; they act out story exactly as it is being read.

NARRATOR: John 20:2-10
"Then Mary runneth and cometh to Simon Peter and to the other disciple whom Jesus loved, and saith unto them, They have taken away the Lord out of the sepulcher and we know not where they have laid him. Peter therefore went forth and that other disciple and came to the sepulcher. So they ran both together and the other disciple did outrun Peter and came first to the sepulcher; and he, stooping down and looking in, saw the linen cloths lying, yet went he not in. Then cometh Simon Peter following him and went into the sepulcher, and seeth the linen clothes lie and the napkin that was about his head not lying with the linen clothes but wrapped together in a place by itself. Then went in also the other disciple which came first to the sepulcher; and he saw and believed. For as yet they knew not the Scripture, that he must rise from the dead. Then the disciples went away again unto their own home."

Exit
PETER and JOHN.

NARRATOR: John 20:11-18
"But Mary stood without at the

MARY sits at far side stage, weeping sadly, head bowed in hands. TWO ANGELS return; both go inside tomb, stand there in open space visible to all.

sepulcher, weeping; and as she wept, she stooped down and looked into the sepulcher, and seeth two angels in white, one at the head and the other at the feet where the body of Jesus had lain. And they say unto her, Woman, why weepest thou? She saith unto them, Because they have taken away my Lord and I know not where they have laid him. And when she had thus said, she turned herself back and saw Jesus.

MARY looks about suddenly, at sound of her name; excitedly.

Jesus saith unto her, Woman, why weepest thou? Whom seekest thou? She, supposing him to be the gardener, saith unto him, Sir, if thou hast borne him hence, tell me where thou hast laid him, and I will take him away. Jesus saith unto her, Mary! She turned and saith unto him, Master! Jesus saith unto her, Touch me not for I am not yet ascended to my father and your father, and to my God and your God. Mary Magdalene came and told the disciples that she had seen the Lord and that he had spoken these things unto her."

Exit MARY.

TWO ANGELS emerge from tomb; stand at either side of open door.

(MUSICIAN plays brief theme from "In Joseph's Lovely Garden".)

Enter TWO ROMAN GUARDS from rear; TWO PRIESTS from one side; meet center stage,

NARRATOR: Matt. 29:11-15 "Now when they were going, behold some of the watch came into the city and showed to the chief priests all

acting out in panto-
mime the story that is
being read. They use
cloth bag and metal
washers for money.
PRIESTS give money;
GUARDS count it out
etc.

the things that were done. And
when they were assembled with the
soldiers and had taken counsel, they
gave large money to the soldiers, saying, Say ye his disciples came by
night and stole him away while we
slept. And if this come to the governor's ears, we will persuade him
and secure you; so they took the
money and did as they were taught."

(PRIESTS AND GUARDS *take several steps to either side stage,
conferring, counting money;* TWO ANGELS *step forward to
front stage, raise right hands, cry,* "HE IS RISEN!" *Guards
drop bags of money with loud clatter, turn in amazement and
kneel before* ANGEL; PRIESTS *also turn in sudden surprise and
fear and also kneel before other* ANGEL *in attitude of rev-
erence.*)

CHOIR: Hymn "The Day of Resurrection" (Tune: Lanca-
shire) (First stanza, unison).

PRIESTS AND GUARDS
rise, exit solemnly,
thoughtfully, to rear of
building.

CHOIR: "The Day of Resurrection" (Third stanza, unison).

TWO ANGELS return to
posts at either side of
open tomb.

Enter CLEOPAS and
COMPANION from
rear; slowly, talking as
they walk; stand deep
in conversation and
thought at one side in
front of stage.

NARRATOR: Luke 24:13-35 (Some
of this may be deleted if time is
short.)
"And behold two of them went that
same day to a village called Emmaus
which was from Jerusalem about
three-score furlongs; and they talked
together of all those things which

had happened; and it came to pass that while they communed together and reasoned, Jesus himself drew near and went with them. But their eyes were holden that they should not know him. And he said unto them, What manner of communications are these that ye have one with another as ye walk, and are sad? And the one of them whose name was Cleopas, answering said unto him, Art thou only a stranger in Jerusalem, and hast not known the things which are come to pass there in these days? And he said unto them, What things? And they said unto him, Concerning Jesus of Nazareth, who was a prophet mighty in deed and word before God and all the people; and how the chief priests and our rulers delivered him to be condemned to death and have crucified him. But we trusted that it had been he who should have redeemed Israel. And beside all this, today is the third day since these things were done; Yea, and certain women also of our company made us astonished who were early at the sepulcher; and when they found not his body they came saying that they had also seen a vision of angels who said that he was alive. And certain of them who were with us went to the sepulcher and found it even as the women had said. But him they saw not. Then he said to them, O fools and slow of heart to believe all that the prophets have spoken. Ought not Christ to have suffered these things and to enter into his glory? And beginning at Moses and all the prophets he expounded unto them in all the scriptures the things concerning himself. And they drew nigh unto the village whither they went, and he made as though he would have gone further; but they constrained him, saying, Abide with us for it is toward evening and the day is far spent. And he went in to tarry with them; and it came to pass as he sat at meat with them, he took bread and blessed it and brake it and gave to them; and their eyes were opened and they knew him; and he vanished out of their sight. And they said one to another, Did not our hearts burn within us while he talked with us by the way, and while he opened to us the scriptures? And they rose up the same hour and returned to Jerusalem and found the eleven gathered together and they that were with them, saying:"

ONE ANGEL steps forward, unseen by the two men; raises right hand and says, when NARRATOR stops,

"HE IS RISEN INDEED!"

CLEOPAS and COMPANION turn, kneel reverently; then rise, exit hurriedly the way they came. ANGEL returns to post beside open door.

CHOIR: Hymn "Christ the Lord Is Risen Today" (Tune: Easter Hymn, unison; all three stanzas.)

(During singing, ENTIRE CAST assembles on stage, in semi-circle about open tomb, coming from different sides of the auditorium, stand, facing congregation.)

ENTIRE CAST kneels reverently; TWO ANGELS hold out-stretched arms over them in benediction.

NARRATOR: Matt. 28:18-20
"And Jesus spake unto them, saying, All power is given unto me in heaven and in earth; Go ye therefore and teach all nations, baptizing them in the name of the father and of the son and of the holy ghost; teaching them to observe all things, whatsoever I have commanded you; and Lo, I am with you always, even unto the end of the world."

ENTIRE CAST Rises slowly, devoutly; all gaze upward at fixed point, as if viewing the Ascension.

CHOIR: Anthem "Unfold Ye Portals" (Gounod) or the Ascension Hymn "Look Ye Saints, the Sight Is Glorious" or any other appropriate selection.

ENTIRE CAST gazes upward.

NARRATOR: Luke 24:50-52
"And he lifted up his hands and blessed them; and it came to pass while he blessed them, he was parted from them and carried up into heaven; and they worshipped him and returned to Jerusalem with great joy; and were continually in the temple praising and blessing God. Amen."

ENTIRE CAST, CHOIR, CONGREGATION sing: "All Hail the Power of Jesus' Name" (Tune: Coronation; first stanza)
(During singing of fourth and fifth stanzas, ENTIRE CAST leaves stage in orderly manner, reverently; NARRATOR stands center stage; motions for all to rise for singing last two stanzas; following the hymn, he dismisses them with the benediction.)

GREAT WOMEN OF HISTORY

A MOTHERS' DAY PAGEANT
by
ERNEST K. EMURIAN

Playing Time: Approximately 45 minutes.

GREAT WOMEN OF HISTORY*

(A Mothers' Day Pageant)

in six scenes

CHARACTERS: 5 men, 6 women; several children and young
people; singers; musicians.

READER
ORGANIST OR PIANIST
CHOIR, or soloists, duet, quartet, etc.

Scene 1: Joseph, Mary, boy Jesus in carpenter shop.
Scene 2: Susanna Wesley, John and Charles Wesley; several smaller
children.
Scene 3: Florence Nightingale; several wounded soldiers in cots in
hospital ward.
Scene 4: Clara Barton; several wounded soldiers on battlefield; Abra-
ham Lincoln.
Scene 5: Fanny Crosby; several young people.
Scene 6: Modern mother with two or three children.

Stage assistants for lights, curtain, costumes, make-up, etc.
If curtain is not available, use moveable screens; or have men hold up
sheets in front of stage when needed.

CHOIR: Hymn, "Happy The Home When God Is There"
(*preferably to tune "St. Agnes"*) (*first stanza*).

(*If time does not permit, this opening paragraph may be
omitted.*)

READER (Proverbs 31:10-31): The author of the Old Testament Proverbs has this to say: Who can find a virtuous woman?
For her price is far above rubies. The heart of her husband
doth safely trust in her, so that he shall have no need of spoil. She
will do him good and not evil all the days of her life. She seek-
eth wool and flax, and worketh willingly with her hands. She
is like the merchant's ships; she bringeth her food from afar.

---

* *Note:* This play is included by permission of THE PROGRESSIVE FARMER,
Birmingham, Ala.

She riseth also while it is yet night, and giveth meat to her household, and a portion to her maidens. She considereth a field and buyeth it; with the fruit of her hands she planteth a vineyard. She girdeth her loins with strength and strengtheneth her arms. She perceiveth that her merchandise is good; her candle goeth not out by night. She layeth her hands to the spindle, and her hands hold the distaff. She stretcheth out her hands to the poor; yea, she reacheth forth her hands to the needy. She is not afraid of the snow for her household for all her household are clothed with scarlet. She maketh herself coverings of tapestry; her clothing is silk and purple. Her husband is known in the gates when he sitteth among the elders of the land. She maketh fine linen and selleth it and delivereth girdles unto the merchant. Strength and honor are her clothing; and she shall rejoice in time to come. She openeth her mouth with wisdom and in her tongue is the law of kindness. She looketh well to the ways of her household and eateth not the bread of idleness. Her children rise up and call her blessed; her husband also, and he praiseth her. Many daughters have done virtuously but thou excellest them all. Favor is deceitful and beauty is vain, but a woman that feareth the Lord, she shall be praised. Give her of the fruit of her hands, and let her own works praise her in the gates.

CHOIR: Hymn, "Happy the Home When God Is There" (*stanzas three and four*).

READER: History records the names of many noble women. Some achieved fame as mothers and wives; others as leaders and pioneers in new and uncharted areas. But the world is better because of the labors and triumphs of these outstanding women. The roll call of heroes and heroines would have to include Maria Mitchell, scientist; Alice Freeman Palmer, Mary Lyon and Emma Willard, educators; Charlotte Cushman, actress; Frances Willard, reformer; Harriet Beecher Stowe, author; Fanny Crosby and Julia Ward Howe, poets and hymn-writers, and countless others too numerous to mention. In selecting the great women of history for this pageant, we are honoring Christian womanhood and motherhood the world over. Through such women as those who will be portrayed, God was at work in different ages of history. Through their modern counterparts, He

94

is still working to make a reality of the prayer, "Thy kingdom come on earth as it is in heaven."

CHOIR: Hymn, "Lord of Life and King of Glory" (*Tune: Sicilian Mariners' Hymn*) (*first stanza*).

(*Curtain is raised, parted, removed, revealing Scene 1; with Joseph, Mary and boy Jesus in the carpenter shop, at work.*)

READER (Matt. 2:19-23): "Now when King Herod was dead, behold an angel of the Lord appeared in a dream to Joseph in Egypt, saying, Arise and take the young child and his mother and go into the land of Israel, for they are dead that sought the young child's life. And he arose and took the young child and his mother and came into the land of Israel. But when he heard that Archelaus was reigning over Judaea in the place of his father Herod, he was afraid to go thither. And, being warned of God in a dream, he withdrew into the parts of Galilee, and came and dwelt in a city called Nazareth, that it might be fulfilled which was spoken by the prophet, that he should be called a Nazarene. (Luke 2:40) And the child grew and waxed strong, filled with wisdom and the grace of God was upon him. (Luke 2:51-52) And he went down with them and came to Nazareth and he was subject unto them; and his mother kept all these sayings in her heart. And Jesus grew in wisdom and stature and in favor with God and man. (*To authenticate carpenter shop scene, see Matt. 13:55; and Mark 6:3.*)

CHOIR: Hymn, "Lord of Life and King of Glory" (*stanzas two and three, as curtain closes on the scene*).

READER: From the pen of the Scottish poet, Elizabeth Cecelia Clephane, has come the beautiful hymn, "Beneath the Cross of Jesus."

CHOIR: Hymn, "Beneath the Cross of Jesus" (*one or two stanzas, as stage is being prepared for next scene*).

(ORGANIST plays hymn tune "Love Divine, All Loves Excelling.")

(*Curtain reveals Scene 2; Susanna Wesley, seated; with her two sons, John and Charles, in clerical garb, standing on either side of her, all facing audience; several smaller children may be seated on the floor, looking intently at their mother.*)

READER (*as ORGANIST continues to play hymn tune very softly*): Susanna Wesley was the wife of the Rev. Samuel

Wesley, a minister of the Church of England, and the mother of nineteen children. Two of her sons, John and Charles, founded the Methodist Church, so Susanna may rightly be called "The Mother of Methodism." "In an age when education for women lay yet in the future, here was a woman who might have talked philosophy with John Locke, or theology with the Archbishop of Canterbury. She has been called by one historian 'the most capable woman in all England'." Daily she directed her children's studies, setting aside an hour each week for the moral and religious training of each child. To the day of her death, her son John consulted her in all important decisions. Few men have owed a mother more. When a fire destroyed their parsonage at Epworth, February 9, 1709, six-year-old John was miraculously saved at the very last moment, rescued by neighbours as the roof collapsed. Mrs. Wesley impressed upon him from that moment that he was a "brand plucked from the burning," and she dedicated him to God anew for the work of His kingdom. Her training of Charles first uncovered his rare poetic gifts, which were to flower into the fruit of more than four thousand hymns, among them the finest in the English language.

CHOIR: Hymn, "Jesus, Lover of My Soul" (*Tune: Martyn; stanzas one and four*).

READER: Among the great women of history Susanna Wesley is second to none. It is not strange that one of England's noblest wives and mothers was the wife of a Christian minister and the mother of the first two Methodist preachers, a devout Christian all her days. The "Love Divine" of which Charles sang was the divine love which early possessed this rare and beautiful spirit, the knowledge of which she passed on to her children very early in their lives.

CHOIR: Hymn, "Love Divine" (*first stanza*).

(*Curtain closes on the scene.* CHOIR *sings last stanza of hymn "Love Divine."*)

READER: From the pen of another woman, Katherine Hankey, comes the gospel song "I Love to Tell the Story."

CHOIR (*as stage is being set for Scene 3*): Hymn, "I Love to Tell the Story" (*one or two stanzas according to the time needed to prepare the stage.*)

(Curtain reveals Scene 3; Nurse Florence Nightingale, lamp in hand, is standing in a hospital ward, in the midst of cots on which wounded soldiers are lying.)

READER: Who is this woman slipping silently through the wards of the make-shift hospital in Scutari? Who is this woman with a lamp in her hand, seeing that the attendants are on duty, and speaking cheering words to her charges? Who is this woman who has left the wealth and comfort of an English mansion for the bloody soil of the Crimea? Who is this strange woman who has turned her back upon the prospects of a brilliant marriage to bind up the wounds of the victims of the battle of Balaclava, thousands of miles from the shores of her British homeland? She is the lady with the lamp, the mother of modern nursing, Florence Nightingale. Born in Italy in 1820, reared in England, presented to Queen Victoria at eighteen, a gay debutante, how is it that she is here? Because, caring nothing for high society, long possessed of a deep desire to bind up the broken bodies of the war-wounded, she chose to become a professional nurse. At thirty-four, she enlisted the support of thirty-seven other like-minded women, secured a ship, filled it with medical supplies, and steamed to the scene of the tragic Crimean War. Under her care the men who had been dying like flies in the vermin-infested camp hopsitals began to recover. The death rate dropped from 40% to a mere 2%! Upon her return to England, $250,000 was raised in her honor by public subscription; she used this money to establish the Nightingale Home for Convalescents. Though an invalid for many years, she lived until the age of ninety, writing books on nursing, advising governments and private individuals on hospital work. Single-handedly, Florence Nightingale raised the standards of the nursing profession to the high place which it enjoys today. Longfellow wrote these lines in her memory:

> "Lo, in that house of misery
> A lady with a lamp I see
> Pass through the glimmering gloom,
> And flit from room to room.
> And slow, as in a dream of bliss,
> The speechless sufferer turns to kiss

Her shadow as it falls
Upon the darkening walls.
On England's annals, through the long
Hereafter of her speech and song,
That light its rays shall cast
From portals of the past.
A LADY WITH A LAMP shall stand
In the great history of the land,
    A noble type of good
    Heroic womanhood!"

From the pen of one of her English contemporaries, Frances Ridley Havergal, comes the poem-hymn which best characterizes the life of the lady with a lamp, "Take my life, and let it be, Consecrated, Lord, to Thee."

CHOIR: Hymn, "Take My Life and Let It Be" (*first stanza; during the singing, curtain closes on the scene*).

READER: Mary Ann Thomson penned the stanzas of one of the most stirring missionary hymns ever written, "O Zion, Haste, Thy Mission High Fulfilling."

CHOIR: Hymn, "O Zion Haste" (*Tune: Tidings; one or two stanzas, according to time needed; as stage is being set for Scene 4*).

ORGAN *plays slowly, softly, chorus of "Battle Hymn of the Republic" (Glory, glory, Hallelujah, etc.)* CHOIR, *softly, "Battle Hymn of the Republic" (first stanza and chorus).*

(*Curtain is raised on Scene 4;* CLARA BARTON, *with large Red Cross banner in her hand, stands amidst wounded soldiers on Civil War battlefield; muskets, tents, etc., complete the setting.*)

CHOIR: Hymn, "Battle Hymn of the Republic" (*second stanza and chorus*).

READER: The life of Clara Barton was one continuous crusade to relieve human suffering. Born near Oxford, Massachusetts, in 1821, and christened Clarissa Harlowe Barton, she is lovingly remembered today as Clara Barton, the founder of the American Red Cross. Possessed of amazing courage and unfailing perseverance, she became the "angel of the battlefield" during the tragic war between the states, 1861-65. After some years as a school teacher in New Jersey, and a clerk in a government office in Washington, D. C. she found herself by losing her life in humanitarian service during the bloody battles of that terrible war. Organizing depots for hospital supplies, serving as a practical nurse, she often risked her own life by establishing make-shift hospitals dangerously near the actual lines of battle. Following the war years, she aided the government in the search for missing soldiers. At fifty, she wrote, "I was never what the world would call even good looking." But there was nothing little about this dynamic "little woman." "What is nobody's business is my business," she often said, and went out to prove it by what she did. At the Johnstown flood, she was there. When quite an old lady she went to Cuba to distribute supplies during the Spanish-American War. In 1881, after nine hard years of campaigning, she organized the American Red Cross; and for the next twenty-three years she directed its growth and disaster work throughout the entire nation. Before her death in 1912 at the age of ninety-one, she wrote extensively and lectured about the subject closest to her heart. She is a living illustration of the truth that helping others is more important than anything else in the whole wide world.

CHOIR: Hymn, "Battle Hymn of the Republic" (*softly, slowly, stanzas 3 and 4, with chorus*). (*As* CHOIR *sings,* ABRAHAM LINCOLN, *in tall hat, dark suit, scarf, hands clasped behind him, deep in thought, walks slowly down the aisle from rear to front of auditorium, crosses slowly in front of stage, and exits down other (or same) aisle, silently, impressively. This dates Clara Barton with this period of American history. Then, when he has gone,* CHOIR *sings, as curtain closes on the scene.*)

READER: As Julia Ward Howe penned her patriotism in the stanzas of her famous hymn, "The Battle Hymn of the Republic," so also did the school teacher and college professor, Katharine Lee Bates, write of her patriotic feelings in a hymn as great, if not greater, "America the Beautiful."

CHOIR (*as stage is being set for Scene 5*) Hymn, "America the Beautiful" (*as few or as many stanzas as are necessary for the next scene to be prepared*).

(ORGANIST modulates and plays hymn tune for "Blessed Assurance.")

CHOIR: Hymn, "Blessed Assurance" (*first stanza and chorus*).

(*Curtain is raised on Scene 5, showing aged, blind* FANNY CROSBY, *hymn writer, seated in an easy chair in the living room of her New York City home, surrounded by some young people from her Church, who are seated or are standing about the room, looking closely at her.*)

READER (*while* ORGANIST *plays "Blessed Assurance" very softly*): Frances Jane Crosby, born in Putnam County, New York, in 1820, was accidentally blinded when only six weeks of age, by the carelessness of an unlettered nurse. Nevertheless she was to become the most prolific writer of hymns, gospel songs and religious and secular poetry in the entire history of Christendom during her lifetime of almost ninety-five years. More than seven thousand religious poems came from her fluent pen during those long, busy years. Her first poem, written when a girl of nine, contains eight of the loveliest lines in all literature:

> "O what a happy soul am I,
> Although I cannot see;
> I am resolved that in this world
> Contented I will be.
>
> How many blessings I enjoy
> That other people don't;
> To weep and sigh because I'm blind
> I cannot and I won't."

Collaborating with her composer-friend, Mrs. Joseph Knapp, wife of the founder of the Metropolitan Life Insurance Company, she wrote her best loved hymn, "Blessed Assurance" and the solo-anthem, "Open the Gates of the Temple." The English poet, Frances Havergal, paid this tribute to the famous author of "Safe in the Arms of Jesus," "Near the Cross," "Rescue the Perishing," "Jesus Is Tenderly Calling," "Saved by Grace" and hundreds of other favorites:

(CHOIR *hums tune "Tell Me the Story of Jesus" during reading of this poem—if time does not permit, this portion, together with the last sentence of the preceding paragraph, may be deleted.*)

"Sweet blind singer over the sea
Tuneful and jubilant, how can it be
That the songs of gladness which float so far
As if they fell from an evening star
Are notes of one who may never see
'Visible Music' of flower or tree,
Purple of mountain or glitter of snow,
Ruby and gold of the sunset glow?
And never the light of a loving face?
Must not the world be a desolate place
For eyes that are sealed with the seal of years,
Eyes that are open only for tears?
How can she sing in the dark like this?
What is her fountain of light and bliss?

O, her heart can see, her heart can see;
And its sight is strong and swift and free;
Never the ken of mortal eye
Could pierce so deep and far and high
As the eagle vision of hearts that dwell
In the lofty sunlit citadel
Of faith that overcomes the world,
With banners of hope and joy unfurled;
Garrisoned with God's perfect peace;
Ringing with paeans that never cease,
Flooded with splendor bright and broad,
The glorious light of the love of God.

Her heart can see, her heart can see.
Well may she sing so joyously;
For the King Himself in His tender grace
Hath shown her the brightness of His face.
And who shall pine for a glow-worm light
When the sun goes forth in his radiant might?
She can read His law as a shining chart
For His fingers have written it on her heart.
She can read His love, for on all her way
His hand is writing it every day.
'Bright cloud' indeed must that darkness be
When 'Jesus only' the heart can see.

Dear blind sister over the sea
An English heart goes forth to thee.
We are linked by a cable of faith and song,
Flashing bright sympathy all along;
One in the east and one in the west,
Singing for Him whom our souls love best;
"Singing for Jesus," telling His love
All the way to our home above,
Where the severing sea with its restless tide
Never shall hinder and never divide.
Sister! what shall our meeting be,
When our hearts shall sing and our eyes shall see!"

CHOIR: Hymn, "Saved by Grace" (*first and last stanzas and chorus, as curtain closes on the scene*).

CHOIR: Anthem, "Songs My Mother Taught Me" (*or as a solo, as stage is being set for Scene 6*).

(*Curtain is opened, revealing Scene 6, Mothers of Today; a modern mother is putting her children to bed, pausing to tell them a story, or read from a story book close by; children are in their pajamas.*)

CHOIR: *Sings* "Home Sweet Home" (*first stanza; then hums the music slowly during the reading*).

READER: So the modern mother takes her place in the line of those heroic and brave women who through all the ages have pioneered and persevered to make the world a better place in which to live. In the office, at the desk, in the factory, in the school room; in positions exalted as well as humble; as the executive as well as the employee. But nowhere is her influence more profoundly felt than in the building of a Christian home. Here she is the queen as well as the cook; the princess as well as the mother; the companion of her husband, the teacher and inspirer of her children; hearing their first prayers, rocking them to sleep with her singing, and from her lips letting them hear their first lullabies, their first lilting songs and hymns; reading to them the beloved nursery stories that have delighted children for generations; and telling them the thrilling and fascinating stories of the Bible, and holding before them always the love of God as we know Him in His beloved Son, Jesus

102

Christ. Combining the best of today with the finest of yester-day, while dreaming and building for a better tomorrow, she is God's handmaiden, a builder of a home where He will be glorified, and, in so doing, engaging in the most trying, most difficult, most exalted and most important job in all the world. We hail the modern mother who is living out the petition from the Lord's prayer, "Thy kingdom come on earth as it is in heaven."

CHOIR: Hymn, "For the Beauty of the Earth" (*Tune: Dix; stanzas one, four, six; as* ENTIRE CAST *assembles on the stage, in a semi-circle, facing the audience*).

(CHOIR, CAST, CONGREGATION, *unite in singing the hymn "Fairest Lord Jesus," all three stanzas; after the second stanza,* CAST *exits in an orderly manner; following the singing of the last stanza,* READER *steps forward and dismisses the congregation.*)

Note: Hymns and song may be added or deleted according to the time available; also scenes may be omitted if time does not permit the showing of the entire series of six. Other minor adjustments can be made as local cases may require. Six different directors may be selected, each one to be responsible for the characters, settings, stage properties, etc., for each scene.

THANKSGIVING THROUGH THE AGES

A THANKSGIVING PLAY
in four scenes

by

ERNEST K. EMURIAN

THANKSGIVING THROUGH THE AGES

by

ERNEST K. EMURIAN

For: 10 men; 4 women; 1 boy; several children; several adults (if available) as extra Pilgrim and Indian families; Musician; Singers; Stage assistants.

CHARACTERS

Scene 1: Aged Priest, with scroll.
Scene 2: Saint Paul, older man; Sosthenes, Aquilla, younger disciples.
Scene 3: Pilgrim, wife, children; Indian Chief, squaw, children; Squanto, Indian friend of Pilgrims; several Indian families (if available).
Scene 4: President Abraham Lincoln; Secretary of State Seward; Mrs. Sara Hale, aged 75; Tad Lincoln, the president's son, 10; Maid.

NARRATOR
ORGANIST (or pianist)
CHOIR (or selected soloists)
STAGE MANAGERS, for lights, changing scenery, curtain.
Costumes and interiors typical of the various eras in history.

Scene 1

The Temple in Jerusalem, about 600 B.C.

ORGANIST: Hymn tune, "Kremser" ("We Gather Together To Ask the Lord's Blessing").

CHOIR: First stanza same hymn.

NARRATOR: From time immemorial the spirit of thanksgiving has welled up within the hearts of thoughtful and sensitive men and women. Long before man knew the name of God, he lifted up his eyes toward the heavens in a gesture of gratitude; or held outstretched arms before an unknown deity as a token of appreciation for benefits conferred, victories won or tragedies averted. Some of the most beautiful expressions of thanksgiving are found in the Psalms of the Old Testament, written several centuries after Moses had given to his people a name for their deity, the name Jehovah. Excerpts from several of these paeans of praise reveal their lofty character and deep spirituality.

CHOIR: Second stanza same hymn.

(Enter: Aged Priest, with scroll in hand; stands in front of curtain, as next scene is being prepared; unrolls scroll and reads these portions, as organist plays softly the hymn tune "Nun Danket" ("Now Thank We All Our God"). (Or, curtain may be raised, showing Priest seated, deep in thought; then he rises, steps forward, unrolls scroll, and reads.)

"Make a joyful noise unto the Lord, all ye lands,
Serve the Lord with gladness; come before his presence with singing;
Know ye that the Lord, he is God;
It is he that hath made us, and not we ourselves;
We are his people and the sheep of his pasture.
Enter into his gates with thanksgiving and into his courts with praise;
Be thankful unto him and bless his name;
For the Lord is good; his mercy is everlasting
And his truth endureth unto all generations. (Psalm 100)
(Brief pause)
Bless the Lord, O my soul, and all that is within me;
Bless his holy name.
Bless the Lord, O my soul, and forget not all his benefits:
Who forgiveth all thine iniquities,
Who healeth all thy diseases;
Who redeemeth thy life from destruction;
Who crowneth thee with loving kindness and tender mercies;
Who satisfieth thy mouth with good things so that thy youth is renewed like the eagles. (Psalm 103)
The Lord executeth righteousness and judgment for all that are oppressed.
(Brief pause)

O give thanks unto the Lord for he is good;
For his mercy endureth forever.
O that men would praise the Lord for his goodness,
And for his wonderful works to the children of men.
And let them sacrifice the sacrifices of thanksgiving
And declare his works with rejoicing." (Psalm 107)

(*Aged Priest rolls up scroll and exits; as* CHOIR *sings first stanza of hymn "Now Thank We All Our God." [Or, Priest may roll up scroll, sit down in meditation as curtain closes on the scene.*])

Scene 2

St. Paul's room in Ephesus, 57 A.D.

NARRATOR: A thousand years after the Psalms were written, men and women were talking about the lamb of God who had been born in Bethlehem, reared in Nazareth and who had preached for three brief years in Judaea, Samaria and Galilee, only to fall prey to the designs of wicked men, who forced him to suffer the cruel death of crucifixion. But God had overridden the schemes of Satan and raised up his son on the third day. Pentecost had followed the resurrection and ascension, and now the infant church was growing faster among the Gentiles than among the Jews. Pioneer missionary, Saint Paul, dramatically converted on the Damascus road, had already completed his first journey with Barnabas, his co-worker; and was now on his second missionary tour. Having visited Europe as the first Christian preacher to that continent, we find him now in the great city of Ephesus, writing a letter to the little church he had established some time before in the Greek city of Corinth.

(*Curtain reveals* PAUL, *sitting at a table in an otherwise rather plain room, furnished with a few chairs, stools, etc.; facing audience, he is writing, reading his lines aloud as he writes them down.*)

PAUL (*reading as he writes*): So when this corruptible shall have put on incorruption, and this mortal shall have put on immortality, then shall be brought to pass the saying that is written, Death is swallowed up in victory. O death, where is thy sting? O grave, where is thy victory? The sting of death is sin, and the strength of sin is the law; but thanks be to God who giveth us the victory through our Lord Jesus Christ. Therefore, my beloved brethren, be ye steadfast, unmoveable, always abounding in the work of the Lord, forasmuch as ye know that your labor is not in vain in the Lord.

(*Knock at door.*)

PAUL: Come in.

(*Enter:* SOSTHENES *and* AQUILLA. PAUL *rises, greets them warmly by name; they shake hands; he motions to chairs and they sit on either side of the table at which he has been writing; he returns and resumes former chair as they converse.*)

SOSTHENES: Paul, Aquilla asked about the meeting in his home tonight. Are you planning to attend?

AQUILLA: The believers hope you will be there, Paul.

PAUL: If I finish this letter I'm writing to the Corinthians, Aquilla, I will surely be present. The church in your house may someday be a stronger church than the one we established in Corinth. Don't you think so, Sosthenes?

SOSTHENES: At least it will be a more harmonious group of believers. In Corinth the people are always taking sides. One says, I am of Paul; and another says, I am of Apollos.

PAUL: And a third answers, But I am of Peter. So instead of one church under the lordship of Jesus, we have three. And the unity of the faith breaks down into a dangerous and terrible diversity.

AQUILLA: So we give thanks to God for the unity of our church here in Ephesus.

PAUL: Amen and Amen. Remind me, Sosthenes, to tell the Corinthians that the church that meets in the house of our beloved Aquilla and Priscilla sends greetings.

AQUILLA: Be sure to include that, Paul. Every church should feel its one-ness with every other church. We in Ephesus need the prayers of those in Corinth and Thessalonica, and if what you said is true, they surely need our prayers too.

SOSTHENES: Have you about finished your letter, Paul?

PAUL (*picking up the sheets on which he had been writing*): Almost.

AQUILLA: What is the burden of the letter, Paul?

110

PAUL: The Corinthian church is so new that many of the members are not deeply and strongly rooted and grounded in the faith. There are factions, lawsuits, immorality; abuses of the Lord's Supper; heresies about the resurrection; false apostles constantly plague them; there is disorderly conduct in public assemblies; and problems about marriage and the place of women in the church.

SOSTHENES: Will you deal with all of those matters in your letter?

PAUL: Hardly, Sosthenes; at least just in broad outline and not in complete detail. (*He hands the sheets to* SOSTHENES *who glances through them quickly.*)

SOSTHENES (*reading*): Thanks be to God who giveth us the victory through our Lord Jesus Christ.

AQUILLA (*thoughtfully, rising to glance at the letter too*): "Thanks be to God—thanks be to God."

PAUL: That is the theme. Thanks for the wonderful love of God, revealed to us in the person of his beloved Son.

(*The other two men resume their seats, watch* PAUL *intently as he talks.*)

PAUL: Thanks in the midst of poverty as well as plenty; in success, but alike in failure; in tragedy as well as in triumph.

SOSTHENES: Did Jesus say that?

PAUL: Not in those words, but they can be read between the lines of his message. Do you recall the incident of his feeding the five thousand?

AQUILLA: Yes. I have told it over and over again.

PAUL: Do you recall his words?

AQUILLA: Well I do, Paul. "And Jesus took the loaves—the five loaves as well as the two small fish—and when he had given thanks, his disciples distributed them to those that were set down."

SOSTHENES: And I remember his prayer, the one that John told us about, after his discourse and woes regarding the cities of Chorazin and Bethsaida, those that rejected him and refused to hear his message. "And Jesus said, I thank thee, O Father, because thou hast hid these things from the wise and prudent and hast revealed them unto babes."

111

PAUL: And again after the raising of Lazarus, how he prayed those words, "I thank thee, Father, that thou hast heard me."

SOSTHENES: And at the Last Supper. "He took the cup and gave thanks and gave it to them."

PAUL: Some day, in another letter or sermon, I want to record these words, with the life and spirit of our Lord in mind, "In everything give thanks."

SOSTHENES: Did Jesus say those words?

PAUL: No, but He lived them. He was not thankful *for* everything. Oh no; the cruel cross was nothing to be thankful for. But He was thankful that in the midst of His sufferings God was still His Father; that in the presence of death, like the Psalmist of old, He would fear no evil, because God was with Him. And I want all of my people to possess the same spirit.

AQUILLA: Thanks be to God. In everything give thanks. That about sums up the law and the prophets, does it not?

PAUL: With one more word added.

AQUILLA: What word?

PAUL (*picking up a scroll nearby and handing it to him*): Read it in Psalm 107; you will find the phrase about half-way through the psalm.

AQUILLA (*finding the place*): Is this it? "And let them sacrifice the sacrifices of thanksgiving and declare his works with rejoicing"?

PAUL: That is it, Aquilla. "The sacrifices of thanksgiving." For this reason, I want to close my letter to the church at Corinth in this manner. "Thanks be to God who giveth us the victory"—followed closely with some definite advice about the collection for the poor in Jerusalem.

SOSTHENES: Is that the proper order, Paul? Is it right to go from the heights of thanksgiving to—

PAUL: To the depths of a collection? Is that what you were going to say?

SOSTHENES (*laughing*): Not exactly; but you know what I mean.

PAUL: I do, son; but I want all my disciples to know that we must always proceed from "Thanks be to God" to "Now concerning the collection." Because the collection for the saints, the poor brethren in Jerusalem, must be received always in an orderly, regular and proportionate manner, in the spirit of gratitude.

AQUILLA: In other words, the collection is one of the "sacrifices of thanksgiving."

PAUL: Exactly. But Sosthenes, go with Aquilla and make ready for the gathering tonight in his home. I will finish the letter. Tomorrow, I want you to gird yourself for a long journey, to take this letter over into Greece to the Corinthians.

SOSTHENES: We will make all the preparations, Paul; and I will be back in time to accompany you to the meeting.

AQUILLA (*embracing* PAUL): Until tonight, God be with you.

PAUL: And with you, too, my brother in the Lord.

(*Exit:* SOSTHENES *and* AQUILLA.)

PAUL (*resuming his writing, reading as he writes, and as curtain slowly closes on the scene*): Now, concerning the collection for the saints, as I have given order to the churches of Galatia, even so do ye. Upon the first day of the week, let everyone of you lay by him in store as God hath prospered him, that there be no gatherings when I come. And when I come . . .

(*Curtain closes on the scene; as* ORGANIST *plays softly hymn tune* "Nun Danket.")

Scene 3

The Pilgrim Colony, Plymouth, Massachusetts.

ORGAN *and* CHOIR: *Second stanza hymn* "Now Thank We All Our God."

NARRATOR: The note of thanksgiving which permeates the Psalms of the Old Testament, has a prominent role in the ministry of Jesus and occupies a large place in the letters of St. Paul. Almost sixteen hundred years after the scene that has just been portrayed, a band of daring and intrepid pioneers boarded a little sailing ship, the Mayflower, to journey to a new land, and there to found a new colony and begin a new nation. On November 21, 1620, the tiny ship dropped anchor in Cape Cod, and the Pilgrims first set foot on American soil. Nearly everyone waded ashore, since the ship's boat was unseaworthy.

About fifteen of the men, well-armed, wandered about the shore, but saw no Indians. The women-folk, after the tiresome trip, insisted upon washing the dirty clothes in a nearby pond. So began the building of a new nation by those motivated by a desire to "worship God according to the dictates of their own consciences." Against tremendous odds the colony continued. Suffering, sickness, privation and death became daily and hourly occurrences. However, near the end of the first year, things began to brighten up for the bold adventurers. But let them tell their story in their own words.

(ORGANIST *plays hymn tune "St. George's, Windsor" ("Come, Ye Thankful People, Come"), as* PILGRIM, WIFE, CHILDREN; INDIAN CHIEF, SQUAW, CHILDREN, SQUANTO *and others enter, either from rear or sides of auditorium, walk slowly to front, and gather in a group in front of curtain on stage, as stage is being set for next scene. The children get together and play with bows and arrows, shooting at a target, or else play in a mock Indian war dance during the scene, informally, as children usually do.) (Or, curtain may be raised, showing* PILGRIM *group at right;* INDIAN *group at left, in colorful settings typical of each group.)*

PILGRIM: When we landed at Plymouth Rock, we were a small company; forty-four men and nineteen women and thirty-nine children. Of this number, only eleven were over forty years of age. Our chief was Captain Miles Standish, who was just thirty-six. Though our land grant was in Virginia, the presence of winter demanded a speedy location where we were. So we changed our plans, put ashore and began to erect shelters and log huts at a townsite named Plymouth on John Smith's map.

PILGRIM'S OLDEST SON: Daddy, you forgot to tell them about the Mayflower.

PILGRIM: That I did, son; suppose *you* tell them about it.

SON: Our ship was called the Mayflower; it was a tiny vessel, just ninety feet long and twenty-four feet wide. There were 102 passengers and 20 members of the crew aboard, so you have some idea of just how crowded we were. We left England on September 16, 1620, and dropped anchor in the new world on November 21, about seven weeks later.

PILGRIM: By March of the next year, 1621, our company was sorely depleted. Severe colds and exposure to the elements had taken the lives of forty-four of our small company. We did manage, though, to build seven log and mud houses. During that first winter we had no clothing but that which was on our backs; most of our food came from the forest or the sea; money was useless in trading with the Indians; we had no neighbours but the savages and no amusements but what we could invent ourselves, and no communications with our homeland save by letters that took months to deliver overseas.

PILGRIM'S WIFE: But we had "courage, a will to work unceasingly, and boundless faith in God."

PILGRIM: Since we arrived too late to plant crops, our daily ration that first winter was five grains of corn. But the Indians, whom we first fought and feared, became our friends and helpers. With their assistance we began to clear the land and plant some crops the next spring.

INDIAN CHIEF: It is true that we feared these white people at first. But gradually through the friendship of Capt. Miles Standish and others we learned to be their friends. One of our tribesmen, Squanto, became the interpreter for the colonists.

SQUANTO: When I was kidnapped by a rival tribe under Chief Corbitant, Captain Standish and his men immediately marched to the new village where I was being kept prisoner, and rescued me and brought me back to my own settlement. Since that brave deed, I have never ceased helping him and his people.

INDIAN CHIEF: Near the end of that first year, Governor Bradford declared "A Day of Thanksgiving." Ninety of my fellow tribesmen joined with me in a three-day festival and entertainment, as guests of the Pilgrims. We tried our skill at arms; and for three days enjoyed the hospitality of our gracious hosts. Our men went out and brought in deer, while the white men brought in enough other fowl to last the entire company a week. There was enough roast deer and turkey for everyone. (SQUANTO *leads the children in games, war-dances, shooting arrows.*)

PILGRIM'S WIFE: Governor Bradford's report on the first Thanksgiving on American soil contained these lines: (*She reads from a paper in her hand.*) "Our corn did well, the barley fair;

but the peas, planted too late, weren't worth gathering. Our harvest being gotten in, four men went fowling. In one day they killed enough to serve us almost a week. Among other recreations, we tried our skill at arms. Chief Massasoit and ninety Indians joined in. We entertained and feasted the Indians for three days. The Indians went out and brought in five deer. By God's goodness we are far from want."

PILGRIM: The second year was filled with misfortune. A terrible drouth withered the corn in the fields; the gardens perished and dried up. After a day of prayer, a ship from home was sighted, loaded with friends as well as supplies. Again the Governor appointed a day of public thanksgiving. And each year thereafter a similar day was enjoyed. However, it was not until 1636, sixteen years after the colony was started, that this celebration became a permanent part of our community life. That year, the colonists met in the meetinghouse, at half past eight in the morning, and continued with psalm-singing, prayer and a sermon until after noontime. Then followed the merry-making and feasting, the poor being the guests of the rich. This type of celebration set the pattern for those that were to come. (*Indian children engage in brief war dance about open fire.*)

(PILGRIMS *and* INDIANS *call their children; and all exit to side or rear of the auditorium, as* ORGANIST *plays hymn tune for* "Come, Ye Thankful People, Come.")

(CHOIR *then sings first and second stanzas of the same hymn while characters for Scene 4 assemble on stage, behind curtain.*)

Scene 4

The President's Office, The White House, Washington, D.C., October 1863.

NARRATOR: Two hundred and forty-two years after the Pilgrims celebrated their first day of Thanksgiving, recreation and feasting, in 1621, a scene took place in the office of the President of the United States in the White House in Washington, D.C., which was to have a profound effect on the observance of Thanksgiving Day in the United States of America. The president, Abraham Lincoln; the time, October, 1863.

(*Curtain is raised, revealing* LINCOLN *at his desk; he is busy writing, speaking some phrases aloud as he writes.*)

LINCOLN (*reading aloud as he writes*): —"government of the *people*, by the *people*—for the *people*—must not perish from the earth—" I'll put that away for future reference; it may have to be altered a bit but the essence of my faith in democracy is summed up there as concisely as it could possibly be anywhere. (*He folds the sheet and places it in a desk drawer, as knock is heard at the door.*)

LINCOLN: Come in.

(SECRETARY OF STATE SEWARD, *followed by* MRS. HALE, *enters the room.*)

LINCOLN: Come in, Seward.

SEWARD (*greeting his chief*): Mr. President, this is Mrs. Sara Hale.

LINCOLN (*shaking hands, pointing to a chair*): Mrs. Hale; how do you do?

MRS. HALE: Mr. President, this is an honor. I hope I am not taking you from more important or urgent work.

LINCOLN (*as they sit about the room*): Not at all, Mrs. Hale. The pressure of these war years is very heavy. I carry a far more burdensome load than any of my political opponents will admit, or my closest friends can share. So it is a welcome relief to spend a little time in the company of the famous editor of Godey's "Lady's Book."

MRS. HALE (*smiling*): How did you know, Mr. President?

SEWARD: There is very little that Mr. Lincoln does not know, Mrs. Hale.

MRS. HALE: I can well believe that, Mr. Seward. Do you actually read my magazine, Mr. President?

LINCOLN (*bursting into laughter*): Hardly, Mrs. Hale. But I managed to look over the calendar for today before going to supper last night. I remembered your name and mentioned it to my wife at dinner. She reminded me that you were the fashion dictator of our society.

MRS. HALE: There is a difference between a dictator and an editor, is there not?

LINCOLN: Agreed, Mrs. Hale; agreed. But you do find your-

self in an enviable position, do you not, editing the Ladies'
Magazine in Boston as well as Godey's?

MRS. HALE: It gives me a chance to do many other things
in addition to promoting the latest styles in women's apparel.

LINCOLN: For example—

SEWARD: The Thanksgiving Day matter, Mr. President.

LINCOLN: Oh yes, I had almost forgotten. Seward told me
that you were the woman who had written to him suggesting a
nation-wide Thanksgiving Day every year.

MRS. HALE: Yes, Mr. President; that is true. Thanksgiving
should be more than a day of thanks for a military victory.

LINCOLN: But military victories are what we need just now,
Mrs. Hale. If we don't begin getting a few more, this war is
liable to drag out for years and years, with more unnecessary
bloodshed and suffering on both sides.

MRS. HALE: True, Mr. President. But if Thanksgiving Day
is to mean to our people what it should mean, then it ought to
be both a holiday and a holy day for the entire nation. When
the North wins a military victory, you set aside a day for
thanksgiving; when the South wins a major battle, another day
is set aside for them. And both sides thank the very same God
for entirely different reasons. God cannot be that inconsist-
ent, Mr. Lincoln. Surely you realize that. So that is why I
have been campaigning for twenty-seven years for a day of
National Thanksgiving that will include all of our people and
all of our blessings. That is the purpose of my visit with you
today.

SEWARD: I wrote Mrs. Hale on September 26, Mr. President,
that I had received her interesting letter and had commended
the same to your consideration.

LINCOLN (thoughtfully): What you say is right, Mrs. Hale;
tragically right. Here we are thanking God for destroying our
enemies, and there they are thanking Him for destroying us.
Seward, where is that proclamation for a day of thanksgiving
that was issued for last August 6?

SEWARD (searching through papers on the desk, finding it):
Here it is, Mr. President.

LINCOLN: Did you read it, Mrs. Hale?

MRS. HALE: I cannot recall, Mr. President.

LINCOLN: Then read it, please, Seward.

SEWARD (*reading from document*): "It has pleased Almighty God to hearken to the supplications and prayers of an afflicted people and to vouchsafe to the army and navy of the United States victories on land and on the sea so signal and so effective as to furnish reasonable grounds for augmented confidence that the union of these states will be maintained, their Constitution preserved and their peace and prosperity permanently restored. These victories have been accorded not without sacrifices of life, limb, health and liberty, incurred by brave, loyal and patriotic citizens. Domestic affliction in every part of the country follows in the train of these fearful bereavements. It is meet and right to recognize and confess the presence of the Almighty Father, and the power of His hand equally in these triumphs and in these sorrows.

"Now, therefore, be it known that I do set apart Thursday, the 6th day of August next, to be observed as a day for national thanksgiving, praise and prayer, and I invite the people of the United States to assemble on that occasion in their customary places of worship, and, in the forms approved by their own consciences, render the homage due to the Divine Majesty for the wonderful things He has done in the nation's behalf, and invoke the influences of His Holy Spirit to subdue the anger which has produced and so long sustained a needless and cruel rebellion, to change the hearts of the insurgents, to guide the counsels of the government with wisdom adequate to so great a national emergency and to visit with tender care and consolation throughout the length and breadth of our land all those who, through the vicissitudes of marches, voyages, battles and sieges have been brought to suffer in mind, body or estate, and finally to lead the whole nation through the paths of repentance and submission to the Divine Will back to the perfect enjoyment of union and fraternal peace."

(MAID *enters, with tray, refreshments; serves coffee and cookies to all, and exits, while they continue conversation.*)

MRS. HALE: It is a stirring document, Mr. President, and a worthy successor to George Washington's proclamation for a day of thanksgiving in 1789, following the adoption of the Constitution and the Bill of Rights.

119

SEWARD: And Washington issued another one in 1795, I believe; after the successful suppression of the disturbances centering about the Shay Rebellion.

LINCOLN: And President Madison did the same in 1815, following the cessation of hostilities that we call the war of 1812.

MRS. HALE: Most of those proclamations were similar to your recent one: giving thanks for a military victory. I feel, as do many other Americans, that Thanksgiving must be more of a national festival, to be observed by all of the people of our great Republic.

LINCOLN: Then you imply that there has been no such thanksgiving proclamation during the last sixty-five years because there has been no war, and consequently no occasion for a military triumph?

MRS. HALE: Exactly. But we should be as thankful during peace as during war; for peace sustained as well as for a battle won.

SEWARD: She is right, Mr. President. I never thought of it in that light before. Then Thanksgiving, like the Fourth of July, would be a festival for the entire nation to share in, rejoice in and participate in together.

MRS. HALE: And for that end, I have written editorials, letters to the governors of the several states and to the presidents, asking them to set aside a national day of thanks, when we might think not only about our wonderful form of government but also about the providential way that that government has been preserved in historic crises in its brief history.

LINCOLN: What of Fillmore, Pierce and Buchanan?

MRS. HALE: Little encouragement, no support. Maybe they thought they reflected the apathy of the people. I rather believe their own lack of enthusiasm discouraged the people. And some of the southern states are afraid that the rest of the nation would impose a sort of a Puritanic festival on them, as a substitute for the usual festivities which they enjoy.

(*Just then* TAD LINCOLN, *the president's 10-year-old son, comes bursting into the room, calling for his father.*)

TAD (*opening the door and rushing into the room*): Daddy, daddy, William said you had forgotten your promise—is that right, daddy? (*Seeing the guests*) Oh, excuse me; I didn't know you had company.

120

LINCOLN (*extending his arms*): That's all right, Tad. You're always welcome. And don't let William give you any wrong notions about your daddy. When I make a promise to my boys, I keep it. But I want you to meet our guest. You know Mr. Seward; but this is Mrs. Sara Josepha Hale.

TAD (*extending his hand, shaking hands with them both*): How do you do, Mrs. Hale? Hello, Mr. Seward. (*They respond.*)

LINCOLN: Mrs. Hale is anxious to have me set aside a day in November for a national Thanksgiving holiday. What do you think of it, son?

TAD: I'm always in favor of a holiday, daddy; you know that. But please don't let it fall on a Saturday or a Sunday. We have those days off already.

MRS. HALE: Tad, I'm anxious for your father to declare the fourth Thursday in November as a day of national Thanksgiving for the entire Republic; and this will be an annual event from now on. Does that meet with your approval?

TAD: Yes, ma'am. Another day from school is always all right with me.

LINCOLN: As well as a feast of turkey for dinner. What boy wouldn't rise up and call the woman blessed who succeeded in this undertaking! But, seriously, son, Mrs. Hale has convinced me that this is what our nation needs, and I am considering doing exactly what she has requested.

SEWARD: By the way, Tad, does the name of Mrs. Hale mean anything special to you?

LINCOLN (*laughing*): She edits a magazine for women, Seward, not boys!

SEWARD: I'm not talking about her magazine, Mr. President. There is something else in my mind. Think hard, Tad. Mrs. Sara Josepha Hale.

TAD (*shaking his head*): I'm sorry, Mr. Seward; but I don't remember ever hearing of her before this afternoon.

SEWARD: But there is one piece of poetry she wrote—when was it, Mrs. Hale?

MRS. HALE: You must be referring to the poem that appeared in "Juvenile Miscellany," about September, 1830.

TAD: 1830? That's long before my time.

LINCOLN (*laughing*): And almost before mine, too, son.

TAD: What is it that you wrote thirty-three years ago that I ought to know something about?

LINCOLN: You have my curiosity aroused now, Mr. Seward. What is it, Mrs. Hale?

SEWARD: Tell them, please, won't you, Mrs. Hale?

MRS. HALE: I'd rather not; but since you insist and since I want Mr. Lincoln to do what I am asking of him, I will oblige. Tad, the poem I wrote thirty-three years ago wasn't supposed to become a famous poem. There is really nothing famous about it. But, to my great surprise, some of the school children began reciting it, and now, I understand, almost every school boy and girl in the land knows it by heart. It's about a girl named Mary.

TAD (*surprised, pointing to her excitedly*): Not "Mary had a little lamb"?

MRS. HALE (*nodding*): Yes, Tad.

> "Mary had a little lamb
> His fleece was white as snow;
> And everywhere that Mary went
> The lamb was sure to go.

(TAD *joins in the next stanza.*)

> He followed her to school one day,
> It was against the rule.
> It made the children laugh and play
> To see a lamb at school."

LINCOLN (*laughing*): Well, I never would have guessed it; not in a million years. (*Rising, extending his hand*) Mrs. Hale, for the author of "Mary had a little lamb" a mere president should do anything. Her wish should be his command. Would that I could write something as simple to be remembered by in the future.

MRS. HALE (*shaking his hand in farewell*): A proclamation setting aside the fourth Thursday in November as an annual day of national thanksgiving would insure that, Mr. President, I can assure you; thank you so much for your time, and your interest. And God bless you as you try to preserve the Union. Goodbye, Tad; it's been nice to meet you and know you.

TAD (*shaking hands*): Thank you, Mrs. Hale; the fellows in school will surely hear about this.

LINCOLN: And he will be the hero of the day, as if being the son of the president isn't enough for any ten-year old! Thank you again for coming, Mrs. Hale. And God bless you in all of your undertakings. Good day.

(ORGAN *plays very softly, the chorus "Glory, Glory Hallelujah" as* MRS. HALE, SEWARD *and* TAD *exit.* LINCOLN *returns to his desk, sits thoughtfully a few moments, picks up his pen and begins writing, reading his lines aloud as he writes them down.*)

LINCOLN (*reading as he writes*): "I do, therefore, invite my fellow-citizens in every part of the United States, and also those who are at sea and those who sojourn in foreign lands, to set apart and observe the last Thursday in November as a day of thanksgiving and praise to our beneficent Father who dwelleth in the heavens." Abraham Lincoln, President of the United States.

CHOIR (*full voice*) Chorus: "Glory, Glory Hallelujah, His truth is marching on," *as curtain closes on the scene.*

NARRATOR: President Lincoln followed his proclamation of 1863 by another in 1864, thus establishing a precedent for the entire nation. Following his untimely death, his successor, President Johnson, wrote, "In conformity with a recent custom that may now be regarded as established on national consent and approval, I do hereby recommend that Thursday, the 28th of November, be observed as a day of national Thanksgiving." And so it remained until President Franklin D. Roosevelt, in 1939, attempted to change the date to an earlier one. His idea encountered stiff opposition. Due to the controversy over the date, the Congress, which up to this time had taken no official action, passed a resolution in December 1941 making the fourth Thursday in November a legal Thanksgiving holiday for the entire nation.

(NARRATOR *may invite the congregation to unite in singing "Come, Ye Thankful People, Come," as the* ENTIRE CAST *gathers on the stage, joining in the singing. Following the last stanza, the people may be dismissed with a prayer or the benediction.*)

COLUMBIA, THE GEM OF THE OCEAN

1843

COLUMBIA, THE GEM OF THE OCEAN

5 men
2 women

CHARACTERS

THOMAS À BECKET, gifted young pianist, singer and actor.
DAVID T. SHAW, his friend, also a young actor and musician.
MR. R. HARFORD, about 40; in whose home the scene takes place.
MISS HARFORD, his 20-year-old daughter.
GEORGE GRAYSON and GRACE FREDERICK, two young friends of Miss Harford.
NARRATOR.

Costumes and interior typical of Philadelphia, 1843.

Scene 1

SETTING: The comfortable living room of the middle-class Harford home, Decatur Street, Philadelphia. The door to the room is at the left. An upright piano is against left stage wall; two windows look out from the back, properly draped. Appropriate pictures on the walls, rugs, comfortable chairs, a sofa, odd tables, and other bits of period furniture complete the setting of the room. As the scene opens, MR. HARFORD and his daughter, MISS HARFORD, are sitting in the room, reading.

TIME: One morning in the fall of 1843.

NARRATOR (*center stage in front of curtain*): In the comfortable living room of their Decatur Street, Philadelphia, home, Mr. Harford and his young daughter are reading, having no idea that before the morning is spent, in their own home a famous patriotic hymn will be written, and composed. It is one morning, in the fall of 1843.

(*Exit* NARRATOR.)
(*Curtain is raised, revealing the scene described above. After a few moments, during which* MR. HARFORD *and* MISS HAR-

127

FORD *are busy reading,* MISS HARFORD *puts her book down, rises, walks toward the window.*)

MISS HARFORD: Dad, doesn't Philadelphia seem awfully dull to you?

MR. HARFORD: Not particularly, dear. Why?

MISS HARFORD: Oh, nothing; only sometimes I get bored just waiting around for something big and dramatic to happen.

MR. HARFORD: Well, you can't expect something especially thrilling to turn up right in your own living room.

MISS HARFORD: No, you can't. But, dad, wouldn't it be wonderful if something really tremendous would happen! Think of the excitement and the way people would be talking about it for days—

MR. HARFORD: Do you have anything in mind?

MISS HARFORD: No, I haven't. But I can dream, can't I?

MR. HARFORD: I suppose so, as long as you don't threaten to set the house afire, just to stir up some excitement.

MISS HARFORD: I think about those pioneer days, and all that happened down at Jamestowne and up at Plymouth Rock—and everything seems too monotonous and commonplace in comparison. Those really were the days, weren't they?

MR. HARFORD (*still reading*): Maybe so, dear, maybe so. But I can't imagine you and your mother shouldering a musket on your way to the spring, or planting crops and harvesting them in all sorts of weather. Better thank your lucky stars that things have progressed as far as they have.

MISS HARFORD: I know you're right, dad, and I would hate the work, but it makes me feel good to imagine myself a famous heroine back in those trying and difficult days.

MR. HARFORD: Speaking of trying and difficult days, you can shovel snow all winter, if you want to keep the front walks cleared and safe.

MISS HARFORD (*still standing by the window, looking out on the street*): Dad, not that. I want to do something thrilling and big and worthwhile—

MR. HARFORD: Oh, I see; a story-book heroine, instead of an everyday one. Well, if it gives you any satisfaction, just keep on dreaming. Only if you ever make up your mind to really *work*, daddy has all the work in the world your little heart could desire.

Miss Harford (*leaning forward to see down the street, after a few moments*): Dad—Dad—there come those two actors I've been telling you about—I'm sure that's who it is—

Mr Harford (*looking up from his paper*): Actors? What actors?

Miss Harford: Yes, it is. Those two actors I told you and mother about just yesterday. Mr. Shaw who is singing over at the Chinese Museum and Mr. à Becket who is acting at the Chestnut Street Theatre.

Mr. Harford: Don't tell me your prayer for a little excitement is going to be answered. That's more than even I bargained for!

Miss Harford: Dad, they're coming up the walk. What can they want with us?

Mr. Harford (*going toward the door*): Maybe some little bird whispered in somebody's ear that a certain lovely young Philadelphia daughter was languishing for something exciting and thrilling on a particularly dull morning.

Miss Harford (*going through the door with him, as they go out to welcome their guests*): Oh, dad, that isn't nice—that's no way to treat your pride and joy!

(*Exit* Mr. Harford *and* Miss Harford.)

(*A few moments later, their voices are heard off-stage, as they welcome* Mr. Thomas à Becket *and* Mr. David T. Shaw *into their home. After* Mr. Harford *has introduced the young men to his daughter, and all have given their greetings, the four come on-stage, the two guests, and* Miss Harford, *followed by her father.* Mr. Harford *shows the two gentlemen to chairs.* Mr. Shaw *sits down on the sofa, and* Mr. à Becket *in a chair near the piano.* Mr. Harford *and his daughter take comfortable seats.*)

Mr. Harford: This is a pleasant surprise, gentlemen. My daughter was just wishing for something dramatic to happen, and what could be more dramatic than the unexpected visit of two handsome and gifted young actors.

Miss Harford (*blushing, embarrassed*): Now, dad, please—

it is the truth that I said something like that, but it was merely an idle wish on the part of a rather bored young lady.

MR. À BECKET: We appreciate your hospitality in letting us in before we explained the purpose of our visit.

MR. HARFORD: Then this isn't a social visit?

MR. À BECKET: Hardly, Mr. Harford. In fact, it is almost as much a surprise to me as it is to you. You see, David—I mean, Mr. Shaw—came into my room just a half hour ago with a very special request.

MR. SHAW: This may sound strange to you, but I asked Thomas to help me out by writing a new song for me.

MR. HARFORD: A new song? What is this, a contest between rivals?

MR. SHAW (*laughing*): Oh, nothing like that. You see, I'm in sort of a pinch. There is to be a special benefit programme day after tomorrow, and the thing isn't shaping up just the way it ought to.

MR. À BECKET: So he came to me and suggested that I prepare a brand new patriotic song especially for that occasion in order to give the program the needed "bang" or "whiz" or whatever they call it!

MISS HARFORD: And did you?

MR. À BECKET: Not yet. That's why we are here. There was so much confusion over in the theatre that neither of us could concentrate. We asked the manager where we could go to find a quiet room with a good piano, and he gave us your name and address right off.

MR. HARFORD: Well, of all things. (*He laughs good-naturedly.*) But we are glad you came, and we now invite you to make yourselves right at home.

MISS HARFORD: About that song; do you have any idea what it is going to be like?

MR. SHAW: I brought him some of my verses, Miss Harford, but he turned up his nose, and turned them down flat!

MR. À BECKET: Rather confusing, isn't it? Turning up and turning down all in one gesture!

MR. SHAW: Maybe my verses deserved it.

MR. À BECKET: They were sorry stanzas, I regret to say.

But since you have that lovely piano, I'm sure we can hammer out something satisfactory.

Miss Harford (*as* Mr. à Becket *goes over to the piano, takes a seat and picks out a few melodies*): Dad, wouldn't it be wonderful if their song turns out to be a national favorite, that will sweep the country like a prairie fire—

Mr. à Becket: It would, Miss Harford, but don't worry about that. We will be satisfied if it turns the trick for David's benefit.

Mr. Shaw (*walking over to the piano and standing by his friend's side*): I'll agree to that one hundred percent.

Mr. Harford: Mr. à Becket, didn't I understand my daughter to say that both of you gentlemen were actors?

Mr. Shaw: Yes, Mr. Harford.

Mr. Harford: Actors! It's positively uncanny—in fact, it's almost unbelievable—

Miss Harford: Dad, what do you mean? What's the matter?

Mr. Harford (*as all three look at him, amazed*): I said that it was uncanny, unbelievable—

Mr. à Becket: What is, Mr. Harford?

Mr. Harford: Your being actors and coming in here to write a new patriotic song—it's positively amazing—the strangest coincidence in all my life.

Miss Harford (*going over to her father's side, worried*): Dad, what is it? Tell me, dad. Are you all right?

Mr. Harford: Perfectly, dear. But don't you see, this has happened before.

Miss Harford: What has?

Mr. Harford: This business of one actor writing a song for another, or someone writing a patriotic song for an actor in trouble, and that song turning out to be famous throughout the land.

Mr. à Becket: Really? When, where, who was it?

Mr. Shaw (*wiping his brow and resuming his seat on the sofa*): Thank heavens. You had me worried for a little while —I'm glad that's settled.

Miss Harford: Sit down, Dad, and tell us what's on your mind.

MR. HARFORD (*as the four take seats*): It is really strange. Why, don't you remember about Joseph Hopkinson?

MISS HARFORD (*as the others shake their heads*): He wrote one of our songs, didn't he?

MR. HARFORD: One of the finest of them all. Listen to those lines:

> "Hail, Columbia, happy land!
> Hail, ye heroes! heaven-born band!
> Who fought and bled in Freedom's cause,
> Who fought and bled in Freedom's cause.
> And when the storm of war was gone,
> Enjoyed the peace your valor won.
> Let independence be our boast,
> Ever mindful what it cost;
> Ever grateful for the prize,
> Let its altar reach the skies.
>
> Firm, united, let us be,
> Rallying round our Liberty;
> As a band of brothers joined,
> Peace and safety we shall find."

MR. À BECKET: And you mean that he wrote those lines for an actor in trouble over a program?

MR. HARFORD: Exactly. It was back in 1798 when he was just about twenty-eight years old. It seems that there was an actor in the city—and, mind you, it took place right here in good old Philadelphia, P.A.—an actor by the name of Gilbert Fox. As I recall, he came to Mr. Hopkinson late one Saturday night and begged him to write a new patriotic song for a concert the following Monday—just about as much time as you men have this morning—

MR. SHAW: And he did it?

MR. HARFORD: Did he? Why he took the music of "The President's March," that someone named Phylo, or Fife or Phoof wrote in honor of George Washington, and wrote out four of the most thrilling stanzas in all American literature.

MR. SHAW: How long did it take him to do it?

MR. HARFORD: Just until the next afternoon. When the singer came by the next day, the hymn was all ready for him. And when he sang it that same night, it went over tremendously. Later on, even President Adams and his cabinet attended the performance in a body, so great was the influence of that song.

MR. À BECKET: And he did it all in one little day—that's beyond me.

MISS HARFORD: He did have one thing in his favor, Dad. His father was also a famous poet and writer of songs, Francis Hopkinson—

MR. SHAW: Who signed the Declaration of Independence?

MISS HARFORD: The very same!

MR. À BECKET: Then that lets me out. My father was neither a poet of renown, nor did he sign the famous Declaration.

MR. HARFORD: But that's no reason you two men can't do it, if Joseph Hopkinson could.

MR. SHAW: Thomas, after all there was Francis Scott Key. He dashed off "The Star-Spangled Banner" in a little time, didn't he?

MR. À BECKET: Yes, but he had the thrill of a battle to give him the inspiration. I could write poetry, too, if I were thrust into the midst of some bloody conflict, and inspired by the devotion and sacrifice of the warriors.

MR. HARFORD: I doubt that, Mr. à Becket. Don't forget that it was in a day of peace and tranquillity that Samuel Francis Smith wrote his poem, "My Country, 'Tis of Thee." A man who wants to write a stirring patriotic song doesn't need a war or the sight of blood to touch off that creative spark. It's got to be something deeper than that.

MR. À BECKET: All right, I agree. But if you had to write such a song, what would you do?

(*Just then a knock is heard at the door.* MISS HARFORD *rises, goes to the door, and welcomes in her two friends,* GEORGE GRAYSON *and* GRACE FREDERICK. *She introduces them around to her other guests, and they all exchange the usual pleasantries, before they are seated.*)

133

MR. HARFORD: George, we are on the verge of seeing a great patriotic hymn composed right in our midst, and right on our piano.

GEORGE: Great. What's it to be about? And who's doing it?

MR. SHAW: Mr. à Becket is the author and composer, supposedly.

MR. À BECKET: That is, if I can get the right subject matter. What would you write about, George, if you had to write a song?

GEORGE: Well, come to think of it, I don't exactly know.

GRACE: I'd select a theme that is already familiar, something like a combination of the flag and our freedom.

MR. HARFORD: Not bad, Grace. What do you say, Mr. à Becket?

MR. SHAW: It suits me.

MR. À BECKET: Anything ought to suit you. After all, you're just going to sing the song, not write it. But I like that. We were just talking about Hopkinson's "Hail, Columbia, Happy Land" and how he wrote it to oblige an actor in need, and the parallel between that experience and our own—

MR. SHAW: Except for the fact that his song became famous, and ours isn't even written.

MR. HARFORD: But getting back to the subject matter. It's like Grace said. Write about something familiar, only give it a new twist, a novel turn to catch the imagination of the public —and you are made!

MR. À BECKET: Something like "Hail, Columbia"?

MISS HARFORD: Speaking of Columbia, haven't you ever thought it strange that we speak of our country in the feminine and some other countries always speak of themselves in the masculine?

MR. SHAW: You mean, like Columbia from Columbus and America from Americus Vespucius?

MISS HARFORD: Yes. And we call our land the mother-country or the mother-land, and some European nations always speak of the father-land.

MR. HARFORD: That may account for all the wars they have over there.

GEORGE: I've often wondered why they can't live at peace.

134

Maybe that's the reason. They think it is masculine to always be fighting.

GRACE: When it is feminine to learn how to get along with one another.

MR. À BECKET: Chalk up another victory for the women. But getting back to what Miss Harford said, they speak of ships as feminine too, don't they?

MR. HARFORD: I believe they do. Now take the "Constitution." Remember what Oliver Wendell Holmes wrote when they were going to take that old ship to pieces not many years ago?

> "Ay, tear her tattered ensign down!
> Long has it waved on high;
> And many an eye has danced to see
> That banner in the sky!"

and so forth, or you ought to know it, if you don't.

GEORGE: You have something there, Mr. Harford; but then, how did they ever get that name "Old Ironsides" if the ship was a "she" and a "her"?

MR. SHAW: Maybe she had a rough old captain who resented all this feminine stuff.

MR. HARFORD: No; it seems that a sailor coined that phrase back in the war of 1812. When the "Constitution" was battling the British frigate, "Guerriere," a shot fell against her sides and bounced harmlessly off. Then that sailor shouted, "Huzza; her sides are made of iron!" And they dubbed her "Old Ironsides."

MR. À BECKET: But getting back to that "she" and "her" again, it may be because it costs so much to keep them in paint!

GEORGE: Or in powder!

MR. HARFORD: That's it, Mr. à Becket; that's it.

MR. À BECKET: What, Mr. Harford?

MR. HARFORD: Your song. We've been talking of the navy and about the army and about the flag at Fort McHenry and about Columbia—why not roll them all together into one song.

MR. À BECKET: Like

> "the army and the navy forever,
> Three cheers for the red, white and blue!"

MISS HARFORD (*enthusiastically*): Yes—yes—that's right—now find the right music—

MR. À BECKET (*turning to the keyboard, as* MR. SHAW *rises and walks over to his side, and the others lean forward anxiously in their seats*): I'll try—but I don't guarantee a hit right off—

(MR. À BECKET *picks out a few melodies, and then, suddenly, with evident inspiration, he finds the music appropriate for his refrain, and sings it with much feeling. Then he turns and speaks to* MR. HARFORD.)

MR. À BECKET: Mr. Harford, give me another verse or two from some other patriotic songs—not those I know, like "The Star-Spangled Banner" or "My Country 'Tis of Thee," but another—maybe they'll help me get started.

MR. HARFORD: There's that verse of Timothy Dwight's:

"Columbia, Columbia, to glory arise,
  The queen of the world and the child of the skies!
  Thy genius commands thee; with rapture behold,
  While ages on ages thy splendors unfold."

MR. À BECKET: That's good. And another—

MR. HARFORD: All right. Now this one's a gem; it's the last stanza of Hopkinson's famous hymn:

"Behold the chief who now commands,
  Once more to serve his country, stands—
  The rock on which the storm will beat;
  The rock on which the storm will beat.
  But arm'd in virtue firm and true,
  His hopes are fixed on Heaven and you.
  When hope was sinking in dismay,
  And glooms obscured Columbia's day,
  His steady mind, from changes free,
  Resolved on death or liberty."

GEORGE: And don't forget to put in about the "land of the free and the home of the brave."

MISS HARFORD: Or better still, reverse the phrase and say

136

"the land of the brave and the free," or "the home of the brave and the free."

GRACE: That's even better.

MR. À BECKET: Now, to scramble them all together and see what comes out. When Mr. Harford spoke of that last stanza as a gem, I thought of these words, "O Columbia, the gem of the ocean," and then added Miss Harford's—"The home of the brave and the free." How is that?

MR. HARFORD (*as all express approval, and enthusiasm for the lines*): An excellent beginning. But make it martial—stirring—almost as if we could see the flags waving and the bands playing and the people marching as the song progresses— And don't be afraid of playing on our emotions—it'll do us more good than harm, believe me.

MR. À BECKET: David, take down these lines for me, will you? I can remember the music but the words may get away before I can write them down.

MR. SHAW: And if the song *does* become famous, then what?

MR. À BECKET (*jokingly*): Then the chances are that you will steal it from me and tell the world that you wrote it yourself.

GEORGE: He can't get away with that. You have witnesses.

MR. SHAW: For which he is profoundly grateful. Now, on with the song.

GRACE: I'll make a copy of the words, too, Mr. à Becket, in case Mr. Shaw loses his—

MR. À BECKET: Or refuses to let me see them, when I forget them—

GRACE: Mr. à Becket, are you any relation to the Thomas à Becket who was Archbishop of Canterbury a long time ago?

GEORGE: The one who was murdered in front of his altar by the king's soldiers?

MR. SHAW: No danger. Thomas hasn't been at an altar since he was christened.

MR. À BECKET: No, Grace; as far as I know, there isn't any connection, but I've often wondered why my parents gave me his name, when he lived about eight-hundred years ago.

MR. SHAW: Maybe they wanted Thomas to have one redeeming feature about him, if it was just his name.

MR. HARFORD: The song, gentlemen, the song; or is this gathering to deteriorate into a genealogical discussion?

MR. À BECKET (*striking several chords on the piano and finding the key he wants, playing a line or so as he repeats the stanzas*):

> O Columbia, the gem of the ocean,
> The home of the brave and the free,
> The shrine of each patriot's devotion,
> A world offers homage to thee.
> Thy mandates make heroes assemble,
> When Liberty's form stands in view;
> Thy banners make tyranny tremble,
> When borne by the red, white and blue.

GEORGE: "Sic semper tyrannis," as they say down in Virginia . . .

GRACE: You know, George, I always thought that meant "Get your foot off my chest," when I saw it on the seal, but that man was killing a tyrant, wasn't he?

GEORGE: Pass it, folks and let's go on with the song.

MR. À BECKET (*as others smile, and watch eagerly, the two still taking down the lines*): I think I'll repeat those lines for the chorus:

> When borne by the red, white and blue,
> When borne by the red, white and blue;
> Thy banners make tyranny tremble,
> When borne by the red, white and blue.

MR. HARFORD (*applauding, as the others gather about the piano, anxiously watching the progress of the song*): Superb—magnificent—if that doesn't go over it won't be the song's fault—

MR. SHAW: But the singer's. I get it. But you can count on my doing the very best possible singing with a song like that!

MR. À BECKET: You'd better, David, or I'll forfeit all rights I have in the piece. (*He begins hammering out the music, in big chords, singing the lines to the chord accompaniment, as*

138

he sings the second and third stanzas, and refrains. The others join with him on the refrain of the last stanza.):

> When war winged its wide desolation,
> And threatened the land to deform,
> The ark then of freedom's foundation,
> Columbia, rode safe through the storm:
> With the garlands of vict'ry around her,
> When so proudly she bore her brave crew,
> With her flag proudly floating before her,
> The boast of the red, white and blue.
> The boast of the red, white and blue,
> The boast of the red, white and blue,
> With her flag proudly floating before her,
> The boast of the red, white and blue.
>
> The star-spangled banner bring hither,
> O'er Columbia's true sons let it wave;
> May the wreaths they have won never wither,
> Nor its stars cease to shine on the brave:
> May the service, united, ne'er sever,
> But hold to their colors so true;
> The army and navy forever,
> Three cheers for the red, white and blue.

(*All unite in singing the stirring refrain, as he plays with full and fervent chords; as they reach the last line, the curtain closes on the scene.*)

> Three cheers for the red, white and blue,
> Three cheers for the red, white and blue,
> The army and navy forever,
> Three cheers for the red, white and blue.

(Curtain.)

NARRATOR (*center stage, in front of curtain*): This song was presented for the first time in public, just two days after it was written and composed by Mr. à Becket. Mr. David Shaw had

139

the honor of singing it since it had been composed at his request for his program. Although intervening years have seen other claims for its authorship, and Mr. Shaw was said to have tried to take all the credit to himself, nevertheless, we believe today that this very popular patriotic song was the work of Mr. Thomas à Becket in its entirety . . . Just as the Americans took the music of one of Britain's national hymns and made it our own in "My Country, 'Tis of Thee," so the British took this melody and idea and wrote their hymn, "Britannia, the Gem of the Ocean." In contrast to the experience of Mr. Hopkinson and his famous hymn of the preceding century, Mr. à Becket made no money on his hymn. But the land of his adoption, he being an Englishman, adopted his song and counts it today as among its finest patriotic airs.

(*Exit* NARRATOR.)

DIXIE

1859

DIXIE

4 men
1 woman

CHARACTERS

DANIEL DECATUR EMMETT, 44; gifted pianist, entertainer, song-writer.
MRS. EMMETT, his wife; singer, and pianist.
JERRY BRYANT, in his early forties; Manager of Bryant's Minstrels.
DAN BRYANT, his brother, two years his junior. Blackfaced and in his costume as a Negro Minstrel end man.
NARRATOR.

Costumes and interior typical of New York City, 1859.

Scene 1

SETTING: The small boarding house room in which Mr. and Mrs. Emmett are living, in Catherine Street, New York. The room is humbly but comfortably furnished, with a large old-style bed against the left side of the room; a piano at the right, just above the door. Other period furniture, odd tables, chairs, etc., complete the simple setting. As the scene opens, MR. EMMETT is sitting by the window, looking out on the city street. It is a dull, dismal morning; for several hours the rain has been pouring down. He seems nervous, jittery, and rebels against being cooped up in his room all day. MRS. EMMETT is sitting in an easy chair, reading the newspaper.
TIME: A rainy Sunday morning, September 18, 1859.

NARRATOR (*center stage, in front of curtain*): September 18, 1859, was a rainy and dismal Sunday morning. Cooped up in their room in a cheap New York City boarding house were Mr. and Mrs. Daniel Decatur Emmett. Mr. Emmett was a member of the famous Bryant's Minstrels. Dan Bryant, and his brother, Jerry Bryant, manager of the troupe, have secured rooms in the same Catherine Street house, on the floor above the Emmetts. It is mid-morning.

(*Curtain is raised, revealing the scene described above. After a few moments silence,* MRS. EMMETT *puts down the newspaper and looks over at her husband, sitting there quietly, gazing out the window on to the rainy street.*)

MRS. EMMETT: Still raining, Dan?

MR. EMMETT (*without taking his eyes off the outside view*): Still at it; and it may last all day. What a day—what a day—

MRS. EMMETT: And our only day off in the entire week.

MR. EMMETT: It would happen this way, wouldn't it? Have you ever seen it fail?

MRS. EMMETT: Cheer up, Dan. It can't last forever. There have been lovely Sundays, haven't there? Now take last Sunday—

MR. EMMETT: It was beautiful, I'll admit, but I wasn't so down in the dumps as I am today. If only the weather would come to suit my moods—

MRS. EMMETT (*laughing*): Dan, you're so quaint. Maybe there are plenty of people who are happy today, who need this rain.

MR. EMMETT: But I'd give my right arm to be 'way down south, where the sun is shining, and the birds singing and the darkies singing in the cotton fields—

MRS. EMMETT: And what wouldn't I give for a big dish of good old southern buckwheat cakes and wild honey—

MR. EMMETT (*rising, walking over to his wife*): Honey, you're all right—you're the world's best— And I'm a lucky man—and I know it— I don't know what I'd do when these "blue" spells come over me if it wasn't for you.

MRS. EMMETT: That's what I'm here for, Dan. That's why I married you. I knew you needed someone just like me to help fill up those tired and empty and weary days. Life can't all be sunshine—and we need someone to share those rainy days with.

MR. EMMETT (*leaning over and kissing her*): I could have looked all over the world and never have found a jewel like you. (*He walks over to the window and stands, looking out, listening to the patter of the rain.*) I wish I were in Dixie—

MRS. EMMETT: Where, Dan?

MR. EMMETT (*turning to face her*): Dixie.

MRS. EMMETT: But you just said a moment ago that you wished you were away down in the sunny south.

MR. EMMETT: I know. And that's what Dixie means.

MRS. EMMETT: I don't remember hearing the word used that way before.

MR. EMMETT (*looking out the window*): The colored folks down on the wharves are always talking about good old Dixie. The way they roll their eyes and look up into the sky when they use that word, you'd think the place was heaven.

MRS. EMMETT: Well, it's a new sort of heaven to me, I must admit.

MR. EMMETT: Seriously, dear, I wish I had enough money to get you out of this old boarding house and buy you a really lovely home which would be all our own.

MRS. EMMETT: With our own servants and our private dining room—wouldn't it be wonderful to have our own dining room? I get so tired eating with a room full of people all the time, with everyone grabbing for the best food first—

MR. EMMETT: Yes, dear; we'd even build a special private dining room for just the two of us. What makes me angry is the thought of that wonderful response we received when we were in Europe. Everyone thought we were the most marvelous entertaining group that had ever travelled on the continent—but when it came to money, they thought differently.

MRS. EMMETT: Do fame and fortune ever go together, Dan?

MR. EMMETT: Maybe not. But we should have cleared enough money on that trip to have made us financially independent for life. Instead of that, we went busted—busted! What's the matter with the world anyway? They applaud you so hard with both hands, they haven't a hand left to go into their pocketbooks with. I'd rather have less applause and more cash!

MRS. EMMETT: By the way, Dan, Jerry said he wanted to see you this morning. I wonder if he's up. I'll call him. (*She rises, goes to the door, calls down the hall.*) Jerry—oh, Jerry—are you up?

JERRY (*off-stage*): Yes. What is it?

MRS. EMMETT: You wanted to see Dan, and he's down here now.

MR. EMMETT: Tell him there's hardly a chance of my running out on him, what with this rain and everything—

JERRY (*off-stage*): Be down in a few minutes. Tell Dan to wait.

MR. EMMETT: Don't worry, Jerry. I'll be here, right here looking out the window and cursing the rain.

MRS. EMMETT (*going by the piano, hitting a few stray chords, and resuming her chair and the newspaper*): Maybe it'll clear off by dinner, and we can take a nice walk this afternoon.

MR. EMMETT (*thoughtfully, reminiscing*): What a life! It's been bands and circuses and parades and minstrel shows and costumes and parades and being before the people all my life. I'd like to settle down as a farmer somewhere and never have to face another audience the rest of my life.

MRS. EMMETT: You'd get itchy feet and be behind the footlights in six weeks' time.

MR. EMMETT: Maybe so; but it would be a wonderful six weeks. When I think of grandfather fighting in the Revolutionary War, and dad in the War of 1812, I wonder if I'll ever do something famous, be a hero—

MRS. EMMETT: You're *my* hero, darling. What other conquests could your heart desire?

MR. EMMETT: I give up—you get me every time—I never have a chance—I surrender—completely, and may I add, unconditionally.

MRS. EMMETT: And how can you forget "Old Dan Tucker"?

MR. EMMETT (*walking over to the piano, sitting down and hammering out a line or two of music*): That was years ago—back when I was fifteen—and there was nothing to it in the first place— (*He strikes another chord, and recites the words, as he plays several simple chords, more as a rhythmic background than an accompaniment*):

(VERSE)   I came to town de udder night,
I heard de noise, den saw de sight;
De watchmen dey was runnin' roun'
Cryin' "Ole Dan Tucker's come to town."

146

(CHORUS)   Git outen de way, git outen de way,
             Git outen de way, Ole Dan Tucker,
             You's too late to come to your supper.

  (VERSE)   Sheep an' hog awalkin' in de pasture,
             Sheep says, "Hog, can't you go faster?"
             "Hush! Hush! honey, hear de wolf growlin',
             Ah, ah, de Lawd, bull dog growlin'."

(CHORUS)   Git outen de way, etc.

(*As he sings, the door opens, and* JERRY BRYANT *enters the room quietly.* MRS. EMMETT *motions him to a chair; he takes his seat as* MR. EMMETT *finishes the song, turns on the piano stool to greet his friend.*)

MR. EMMETT: Hello, Jerry. What brings you around on such a perfect morning for sleep?

JERRY: Just what you were doing there, Dan.

MR. EMMETT: What do you mean, Jerry?

JERRY: Another new song.

MR. EMMETT (*rising*): You mean you have the nerve to come down here on a gloomy, dismal rainy Sunday morning and ask me to write another new song. Of all the colossal nerve!

JERRY (*smiling, good-naturedly*): How old were you when you wrote that Dan Tucker piece?

MR. EMMETT: Fifteen.

JERRY: And how long did it take you?

MR. EMMETT: I don't remember.

MRS. EMMETT: You do too, Dan; you told me you wrote it in fifteen minutes.

MR. EMMETT: Oh, all right; fifteen minutes.

JERRY: Well, if you could write a song in fifteen minutes when you were fifteen, what's to keep you from writing a song in forty-four minutes when you're forty-four?

MR. EMMETT (*throwing up his hands in despair*): Of all the foolish ideas, that is undoubtedly the worst I have *ever* heard!

JERRY: Well, what's to prevent it? All your ranting and

147

raving hasn't told me why such a thing should be so impossible. You're the great Daniel Decatur Emmett, aren't you?

MR. EMMETT (*pulling himself up to his full height*): Yes, Jerry, I am the great Daniel Decatur Emmett. What of it?

JERRY: If that man Decatur, after whom you are middlenamed, could say in that famous toast of his, "My country—may she ever be right, but right or wrong, my country!" or something like that, then why can't you say, "My genius—may she ever flourish—but rain or shine, my genius can turn the trick!"

MR. EMMETT: No connection whatsoever—absolutely insane—gone completely crazy— (*Turning to face him*): What would that song be about, anyway?

JERRY: Now that it's raining, I'd say it ought to be about the sun shining on the cotton fields, and little children playing in the sand in front of the little cabin door.

MRS. EMMETT: Jerry, as much as I love Dan, I know he isn't a second Stephen Foster.

JERRY: Maybe not. But what's Foster got that you haven't? Is he happily married? No. Has he travelled in Europe? No. Is he a member of the famous Bryant's Minstrels, playing nightly to capacity houses in the greatest city in the nation? No.

MR. EMMETT: All right, Jerry. Cut it out. That's all I can stand for the present. Now calm down and tell me the sort of a song you want. (*He resumes his seat on the piano stool.*)

JERRY (*rising, walking slowly back and forth across the room*): I want a good walk-around that has a lots of zip to it—a lot of hooray-ing and hurrah-ing—and something that will strike deep at the hearts of these self-satisfied New Yorkers.

MRS. EMMETT: Dan was just saying that he wished he were way down south in Dixie. What's wrong with that?

JERRY (*excitedly*): Absolutely nothing! Absolutely nothing!

MRS. EMMETT: Jerry, before Dan writes that song—

MR. EMMETT: Before I write that song? You folks surely take me for granted. What do you think I am anyway?

JERRY: A genius, Daniel, a genius.

MRS. EMMETT (*as her husband turns and picks out melodies*

on the piano, half-heartedly): Jerry, before he writes the song, tell me what Dixie means, please?

JERRY: Why it means the south, doesn't it?

MRS. EMMETT: I don't know. That's why I asked you. Does it?

JERRY (*sitting down*): I thought it did. Doesn't it, Daniel?

MR. EMMETT (*nodding his head*): That's what the colored folks out on the wharves and on the big farms say.

JERRY: How come?

MR. EMMETT (*still picking at melodies on the piano*): One of them told me that those two surveyors, Mason and Dixon, began the whole thing when they made their "line" back about a hundred years ago. North of that line they can't have slaves, now; and south of it, they can. And they say that the word Dixie came from that man Dixon, when the people couldn't remember exactly what his name was.

JERRY: Sounds tall to me.

MRS. EMMETT: Me, too. But why should a man born in Ohio, and now living in New York City write a song about the south, when he's never lived there?

JERRY: That's not the point. Folks love the romantic stuff about the deep south, and the handsome gentlemen with their courtly manners and mint juleps and big plantations and colored folks singing in the moonlight—

MR. EMMETT: But, Jerry, you forget that I come from Ohio where they don't have slaves, and my father is an ardent abolitionist, and even a member of the "underground railroad" helping slaves to escape from that "heaven" of yours.

MRS. EMMETT: And with all that northern background, you want Dan to write a song about the south?

JERRY: I don't care a snap about background. If the song goes over, we are made, slavery, south, abolition or what have you.

MR. EMMETT: And if it doesn't?

JERRY: I'll just order you to produce another one by the following week, or fire you.

MR. EMMETT: I don't doubt that in the least.

(*A knock is heard at the door.*)

MR. EMMETT: Come in.

149

(*The door opens, and in steps* DAN BRYANT, *blackfaced, and in his full minstrel uniform as an end man. He steps quickly into the room, shuts the door, and gives a courtly bow, shouting, in imitating a band, "Da Dum—" with much fanfare, following that with, "Gentlemen, be seated."*)

JERRY: Dan, what's all this about?

DAN: (*in Negro dialect*): Boss, I'se heard about this here composer Dan Emmett and I was wondering if he couldn't write me a brand new song to sing tomorrow night when that thar minstrel show opens up at Mechanics' Hall?

MR. EMMETT: I give up. If that isn't a friendly frame-up, I've never seen one. First it's Jerry, white, and now it's Dan, black. Pretty soon an Indian will come whooping it up down the hall, threatening me with a scalping if I don't come through with that new song!

DAN (*as all burst into hearty laughter, and take seats*): That's it, Mr. Emmett; that's it!

MR. EMMETT: Dan, I'll write that song about Dixie on one condition.

JERRY: What's that?

MR. EMMETT: That Dan tells us where that word Dixie came from in the first place.

DAN (*thoughtfully*): Well, boss, as I understands it, there's two modern theories about the origin of that very unusual word. In the first place—

MRS. EMMETT (*interrupting*): Is this an answer by a minstrel man, or a lecture by a college professor?

DAN: Neither, Ma'am. It's an humble opinion by your humble servant. And as I was saying: Firstly (*he speaks with dramatic explanatory gestures*): It is said to have originated down New Orleans way, from a French word current among the large French population there, the word "dix," or what we would call "a ten-spot," a "ten franc note."

MR. EMMETT: And?

DAN: And the folks that had those "dix-es" were gradually known as the Dixies, and the place where the Dixies who had those dix-es lived was known as Dixie.

MR. EMMETT (*shaking his head*): Too far-fetched for me. What about you, honey?

MRS. EMMETT: I agree. It's a bit too strong to swallow. Try again, Dan, or no song!

DAN: But the second theory is more likely to be the true one. It seems that a long time ago there lived on Manhattan Island of this noble state of New York one well-to-do kindly farmer, named Mr. Dixie.

JERRY: Now we're getting somewhere. (*The others nod in approval.*)

DAN: Now this Mr. Dixie was reputedly a very good man, who loved his slaves and treated them with utmost respect. But along about the year 1822, when he saw that this state of New York was to pass a bill outlawing the holding of slaves, he shipped his slaves down south, and sold them to southern plantation owners.

MRS. EMMETT: And what happened to them?

DAN: Well, whoever bought them down south didn't treat them like Mr. Dixie had, so the slaves would always be talking about Mr. Dixie's land as heaven. "If we could only get back to Mr. Dixie's," they'd say, until all over the south, in these thirty-seven odd years that have intervened, the word Dixie spread, and everyone who heard of it knew that it meant "heaven."

JERRY: And the southerners, knowing a good thing when they heard it, told the slaves that Dixie was none other than all the land lying south of the Mason-Dixon line, and east of the Mississippi River.

MR. EMMETT: And there you have it; and you have me in three different directions: from the French in New Orleans and their "dix-es" to Mr. Dixie up here in New York state and down to Mr. Dixon the surveyor, in between, none of whom represent the solid south.

MRS. EMMETT: The irony of it all! And now a northern abolitionist will extol the virtues of that lovely land in his new song, Dixie.

(*At this point, DAN BRYANT leaps to his feet, and dances as he sings the first stanza and chorus of Stephen Foster's "De Camptown Races." When he finishes, the others burst into applause, and the dancer bows graciously.*)

DAN: Yas, Mr. Bones. Dat wa'n't no lady you seen me with last night—dat was mah wife—hah, hah, hah—

JERRY (*holding his nose with his fingers*): Deliver me. If he wasn't my brother, I'd fire him! (*And to* MR. EMMETT): And if you can't do any better than Foster in that song, I'll fire you! And that's no joke—

MR. EMMETT: Well, take Dan and get out of here and I'll see what I can do. By the way, should the song become famous, who will get the credit?

DAN: Why, Bryant's Minstrels, of course!

JERRY: Of course not! I'll claim it, since I was the one who made you write it.

MRS. EMMETT (*rising, going to the door with her two friends*): No. I'll settle the argument and claim the honor myself, since I'll have to listen to its being composed, if that is proper English.

DAN: It may not be good English, but it sure is a bad idea! Hah,hah—

JERRY (*at the door*): Come on, Dan, before you drive these people out of their heads. Emmett's got work to do—

MRS. EMMETT: And on a rainy, dismal and gloomy Sunday morning. What better inspiration for a great song!

DAN: So long, folks; we'll be back—

JERRY (*looking at his watch*): Yes; in forty-four minutes.

MR. EMMETT (*picking up a song book from the piano and throwing it at them*): Get out—and stay out.

(*Exit* JERRY BRYANT *and* DAN BRYANT, *as all four burst into long and hearty laughter. When they are gone,* MRS. EMMETT *resumes her chair and browses through the paper.* MR. EMMETT *sits at the piano and picks out different melodies, shaking his head with disgust at each line.*)

MR. EMMETT (*at the piano*): The army was never like this —nor the print shop—nor even my childhood music lessons!

MRS. EMMETT (*reading the paper*): Dan, it says here that some man over in Europe is writing a book proving that it took millions of years for God to create the world.

MR. EMMETT: Well, the six days of the Bible are good enough for me.

> "Dis worl' was made in jiss six days
> And finished up in various ways—"
> Hoorah—hoorah—

152

No, that won't do it— Hooray—hooray— Look away— That's it—that's it, dear, look away—look away—look away in Dixie land. (*Turning to face his wife*): I won't use Dixie's land, but just plain Dixie land. Isn't that better?

MRS. EMMETT (*nodding*): Of course.

MR. EMMETT: But what about the music? I don't know where to start.

MRS. EMMETT: Always start with something good. Now take the song about the Bombardment of Fort McHenry. Play the first line of "The Star-Spangled Banner."

MR. EMMETT (*playing the first line of the music*): All right; where do I go from here?

MRS. EMMETT (*rising, putting the paper down and reaching for her wraps*): Use those notes as a starting point, and take it from there— I know you well enough to know you do your best work alone. So I'm going for a walk while you finish the song.

MR. EMMETT (*rising, helping her put on her coat*): Isn't it raining too hard for you?

MRS. EMMETT (*going to the window and looking out*): It isn't quite as bad as it was earlier. I think I can stand it. Goodbye—and make that song good.

MR. EMMETT (*kissing her, and opening the door for her*): Goodbye. Don't get wet! The song isn't worth it, you know.

(*Exit* MRS. EMMETT *through the door at the right*.)

MR. EMMETT (*getting paper and pencil and a sheet of music manuscript paper, resuming his seat at the piano and picking out words and music at the same time, speaking his lines aloud as he picks them out and writes them down*):

Look away, look away, look away, Dixie land.

(*He then picks out the music and sings the first phrase of The Star-Spangled Banner: "Oh, say can you see," following that with his own words and music for the first stanza of Dixie, "Dis' worl' was made in jiss six days," and nods his head in approval. He continues to pick out the music and sings through the first stanza and composes the chorus spontaneously as he goes along.* OFF-STAGE *banjo player can take*

153

I wish I was in de lann ob cotton,
Ole times darr am not forgotten,
Look away, look away, look away, Dixie land;
In Dixie lann whar I was bawn in,
Arly on one frosty mawnin',
Look away, look away, look away, Dixie land.

In Dixie lann de darkies grow,
If white folks only plant deyre toe;
Look away, look away, look away, Dixie land;
Dey wet de grown wid bak-ker smoke,
Den up de darkies heads will poke,
Look away, look away, look away, Dixie land.

I used to hoe an' dig de lann,
But work dey say am contribann,
Look away, look away, look away, Dixie land;
Driber he come pokin' 'bout,
When massa sole me out-an'-out,
Look away, look away, look away, Dixie land.

Ole missus die—she took a decline,
Her face was de color ob bacon-rhine:
Look away, look away, look away, Dixie land;
To kingdom kum den let 'er go.
For here on earth she stood no show;
Look away, look away, look away, Dixie land.

Buckwheat cakes wid cornmeal batter
Makes you fat or a little fatter:
Look away, look away, look away, Dixie land;
Den here's a health to de next ole missus,
An' all de gals dat want to kiss us;
Look away, look away, look away, Dixie land.

Den hoe it down an' scratch yoa grabble,
To Dixie lann I'm boun' to trabble;
Look away, look away, look away, Dixie land;
Whar de rake an' hoe got double trigger,
An' white man jiss as good as nigger!
Look away, look away, look away, Dixie land.

(*He turns to the piano and plays and sings full voice and with much fervor, the chorus of his new song, as* OFF-STAGE *banjoist plays with him*):

Den I wish I was in Dixie! Hooray! Hooray!
In Dixie land we'll take our stand
To lib an' die in Dixie;
Away! away! away down south in Dixie!
Away! away! away down south in Dixie!

(*As he sings the last line of the chorus, the* CURTAIN *closes on the scene.*)

NARRATOR (*center stage in front of curtain*): The new song by Dan Emmett had its first performance the next night, Monday, September 19, 1859, in Bryant's Minstrels, and became immediately popular. The south adopted it as an official song, though written by a northern boy and first sung in New York City. Unfortunately, the author and composer was criticized and upbraided in the North for his supposed disloyalty to the Union cause. And, until the Civil War was over, he had a hard time making a living. He finally retired to a small farm at his birthplace, Mount Vernon, Ohio, where he lived with his family, in seclusion for many years. Although the composer was almost lynched in the North for his supposed southern sympathies during that bloody conflict, he lived to see his song win universal acclaim. He said, later, "If I'd known it was going to be so popular, I'd have written it better."

He was brought before the public again in the 1890's by a protégé of his, Al Field, the minstrel man, and won thunderous applause in the South. This also replenished his income, which made his declining years more comfortable. He died in Mount Vernon, Ohio, June 28, 1904, in his 88th year. But the song he was ordered to write as a walk-around has sung itself around the world.

(*Exit* NARRATOR.)

AMERICA THE BEAUTIFUL

AMERICA THE BEAUTIFUL*

5 women
Organist or Chorus

CHARACTERS

KATHARINE LEE BATES, 34; attractive, gifted college professor.
THREE FELLOW-TEACHERS, Jane, Alice and Mary, all in their late
    twenties or early thirties.
NARRATOR.
OFF-STAGE ORGANIST or CHORUS.

Costumes and setting typical of western United States, 1893

Scene 1

SETTING: The comfortable living room of the home in which Miss
Bates is spending the summer, in Colorado Springs, Colorado. The room
is warmly, comfortably furnished. Two windows, properly draped, look
out from back stage wall; between them, there is a sofa; on either side
of the room are comfortable chairs, a bookcase or two, other appropriate period furniture, pictures and decorations. A small table is placed
at the left, behind which Miss Bates sits, writing, examining papers, and
making notes. She sits partly facing the audience and partly facing the
opposite side of the stage, where the door to the room is located. As
the scene opens, Miss Bates is alone in the room, writing.

TIME: One evening in the early summer of 1893.

NARRATOR (*center stage in front of curtain*): Katharine
Lee Bates was born on August 12, 1859, in the little village of
Falmouth, Massachusetts. Her father, William Bates, was a
minister of the Congregational Church; her mother, a graduate
of Mount Holyoke. Katharine was reared in this intellectual
and deeply spiritual atmosphere. It was perfectly natural for
her to seek a college education, so she entered Wellesley in

Note: This play is included by permission of THE PROGRESSIVE FARMER,
Birmingham, Ala.

1876, securing the coveted Bachelor of Arts degree just four years later. After a few years of teaching in two different educational institutions, she returned to her Alma Mater, Wellesley, as instructor in English. Following the winning of her Master's Degree at Oxford, she was advanced to the position of full professor in 1891. Two years later, in the early summer of 1893, with a group of fellow-teachers, she travelled west, to spend the summer teaching in Colorado Springs, Colorado. Enroute, the party visited the Chicago Columbian Exposition, which impressed them profoundly. Once in Colorado, the teachers made the trip up famous Pike's Peak and were deeply moved by the magnificent view from that historic mountain top. This scene takes place in the living room of the home in Colorado Springs, where Miss Bates is living during her stay in that city. As the scene opens, we see Miss Bates at her table, writing. It is early evening, in the summer of 1893, her 34th year.

(*Exit* NARRATOR).

(*Curtain rises, revealing the scene described above. For a few moments,* MISS BATES *is busily engaged in writing. After a while, she looks up thoughtfully and recites some of the lines she has just written down.*)

MISS BATES (*looking up from her papers, speaking slowly, reverently*): America, America, God shed His grace on thee;
And crown thy good with brotherhood, from sea to shining sea.

(*She resumes her writing, reading the lines slowly as she writes.*)

MISS BATES: O beautiful for pilgrim feet
Whose stern, impassioned stress
A thoroughfare for freedom beat
Across the wilderness.

(*There is a knock at the door.* MISS BATES *looks up; calls "Come in." The door opens and* JANE *enters the room.*)

JANE (*entering the room, crossing over to the other side*): Oh, Katharine, I didn't know you were busy. What is it now? Another poem?

MISS BATES (*looking up, smiling, motioning to a chair at her*

160

left, which JANE *takes*): Why, hello, Jane. Yes, it's another poem. Why?

JANE (*sitting down so as to face the audience and* MISS BATES): Oh, nothing. But haven't we had enough for today?

MISS BATES (*sitting back in her chair*): I suppose so. But you know how we writers are—

JANE: Don't I! When the mood seizes you, you must write. If you don't, soon the magic spell will depart from you, and your great creative efforts will not have been put down on paper for all posterity to ponder upon and enjoy. (*She bursts out laughing, as* MISS BATES *laughs with her.*)

MISS BATES: All right, Jane. All right. But there is more to that "mood" and "creative spark" than you think. And who can tell about posterity? Maybe posterity will rejoice that I used that spark to kindle a flame this particular time. At least, let's hope so!

JANE (*kicking off her shoes, straightening out her legs and wiggling her toes*): Honestly, Katharine, haven't we had enough? That climb up Pike's Peak almost killed me. My poor feet will never be the same again.

MISS BATES: I ache almost as much, and if I gave in to my physical feelings right now, I'd take a hot bath and go straight to bed—

JANE: Where we all belong! Katharine, who was this fellow Pike anyway? Was he the first man to climb the peak or did he just discover it one day when he was out hunting?

MISS BATES: The only reason I happen to know is that I read through the literature they gave me this morning before our climb.

JANE: I never read the stuff. I'd rather see the real thing than a picture any day.

MISS BATES: Well, the pamphlet said that this peak was discovered by a famous American general and explorer, Zebulon Montgomery Pike, somewhere about 1806.

JANE: And how high is it?

MISS BATES: About three miles, I believe, above sea level; a little over fourteen thousand feet would be more exact.

JANE: That is high enough for me.

MISS BATES: Jane, wasn't that view magnificent?—it really

took my breath away—tall mountains receding in the distance, farther and farther, until the last one seemed to melt right into the misty blue of heaven.

JANE (*laughing*): Say, you're doing all right. Go on!

MISS BATES: Oh, I was just thinking of the comparison between the Chicago Exposition, fashioned by the hands of men, and the splendor of the Rocky Mountains, fashioned by the hand of God.

(*Just then another knock is heard at the door. MISS BATES calls, "Come in." The door opens and MARY enters, dressed in her bathrobe and slippers. When they see her, the other two burst into laughter, while MARY stands there, just inside the room, staring at them. After a moment, MISS BATES speaks.*)

MISS BATES: Come in, Mary; I thought Jane had suffered enough from our exploration of the day, but you seem to have been a worse casualty.

MARY (*sitting down on the sofa, leaning over and rubbing her feet*): Laugh if you will, but this is no laughing matter; I ache, and when I say I ache, I *really* ache!

JANE: But it was worth it, wasn't it, Mary?

MARY: A thousand times. But, what a price to pay to gaze upon the grandeur of nature. Nature in the raw surely made my feet raw!

JANE: And while you were suffering, Katharine was writing another poem about the glorious adventures of the day.

MARY: Katharine! Not another one already!! Where do you find the strength?

JANE: It's not strength, Mary; it's the inspiration. It seems as if the inspiration carries with it the necessary strength.

MISS BATES: Mary, what Jane just said in jest is really the truth.

MARY: Honestly, Katharine?

MISS BATES: I'm not joking, Mary. Just "gazing in wordless rapture over the expanse of mountain ranges and the sealike sweep of the plains" opened the flood gates of my heart, and these lines just poured out as fast as I could write them down.

MARY: Read a stanza, won't you?

MISS BATES: All right, if you two will be sympathetic and not *too* critical. (*Picking up a sheet of paper, she reads.*)

162

O beautiful for spacious skies,
For amber waves of grain,
For purple mountain majesties
Above the fruited plain!
America! America!
God shed His grace on thee
And crown thy good with brotherhood
From sea to shining sea!

MARY (*quietly*): Katharine, that's wonderful—wonderful. "And crown thy good with brotherhood, From sea to shining sea."

JANE: How did those lines happen to come to you, Katharine?

MISS BATES: Jane, I've been thinking a long time about this America of ours. It is a great nation; but is it a good nation? It isn't enough just to be great. Rome was great, but she was not good; therefore, she fell. The Spanish Empire was great in wealth, but morally rotten; it came tumbling down, too. Is there any danger that our own beloved America will follow the same path: thinking she is good merely because she is great? Or must she learn that greatness of the hand, the mind, the mart and mint are not enough unless they make of us a nation of good men and women, good way down within our individual hearts?

MARY: You mean that unless we crown our good with brotherhood, that unless we use what we have for the glory of God, then what we think is good will turn to evil?

MISS BATES: Yes, that's it. We must match the greatness of our America with the goodness of personal Godly living.

JANE: Go on, Katharine. I see what you mean. You're right.

MISS BATES: Think of the Chicago Exposition we saw just a few weeks ago. Has there ever been anything like it in American history?

JANE: I doubt it.

MARY: No, there hasn't been anything quite as vast and pretentious in the last two hundred years. Why?

MISS BATES: If we can produce such magnificent buildings,

163

with such beauty and grandeur, we have the power and the ability to produce a more Godly civilization. The Fine Arts Building alone was a masterpiece of design and construction and physical beauty. But that isn't enough. Unless we produce good citizens, all that splendor is of no avail. Unless we struggle toward godliness and Christian brotherhood, the things we create to bless will, in the end, curse.

(*Again, there is a knock on the door.* MISS BATES *calls, "Come"; the door opens and* ALICE *enters. She greets each of her three friends and then takes a comfortable chair near the door.*)

MARY: Alice, Katharine is discussing her new poem, the one inspired by our visit to Pike's Peak today.

ALICE: Good, Katharine; good for you. As for me, I'm so worn out I couldn't write a line of poetry if my life depended on it. But I'm glad one of us can!

JANE: Katharine read for us the first stanza and just finished explaining it.

ALICE: You have the second stanza ready, Katharine?

MISS BATES: The first four lines.

MARY: Read them, if you don't mind.

MISS BATES: Not at all. (*Reading*):

> O beautiful for pilgrim feet
> Whose stern impassioned stress
> A thoroughfare for freedom beat
> Across the wilderness.

ALICE: And how did those lines come?

MISS BATES: Easily enough. There are two famous stones in history, Alice. You're the history teacher. Tell us about them.

ALICE: Well, Plymouth Rock ought to be one of them.

MISS BATES: Good. And the other? Its date is almost as far before Christ as Plymouth Rock is Anno Domini.

ALICE: Oh; you mean the stones on which Moses carved the ten commandments.

MISS BATES: Yes. If we could couple the daring of the Pilgrims and the moral teachings of Moses, together with the ability of both of them to venture into uncharted seas, we would really have something in this America that no one could ever take from us.

ALICE: Modern Pilgrims. Is that it?

JANE: That's right. There are many seas needing modern pioneers. The seas of ignorance, superstition, greed, lust, selfishness, intemperance. Didn't Lowell write a poem along that line? You're the literature specialist, Mary. What did Lowell say?

MARY: "Lo, before us gleam her camp-fires,
        We ourselves must Pilgrims be:
        Launch our Mayflower and steer boldly
        Through the desperate winter sea;
        Nor attempt the future's portal
        With the past's blood-rusted key!"

MISS BATES: That is the spirit of this second stanza. While we praise the ancient pilgrim, we plague the modern pilgrim. That must stop. It is neither Christian nor democratic. We must be as daring in our pioneering as were they. And as certain of our port, and our Pilot.

JANE: What about the other stanzas, Katharine. Will there be others?

MISS BATES: Yes, Jane. I want to write a stanza about heroes and one about patriots.

MARY: Speaking of heroes, I wish you would tell the world that there are plenty of unsung heroes today, trying to make America great. Too many people think of a hero as a man who is willing to die for his country. I like to think of a hero as a man or a woman who is willing to *live* for America.

ALICE: Sometimes it is much easier to die for one's homeland, than to live for her, isn't it?

MISS BATES: True enough, Alice. When I think of our national heroes, or our heroines, for that matter, I immediately think of military leaders.

JANE: Or Molly Pitcher of the Revolutionary War and Barbara Frietchie of the Civil War.

ALICE: Who was she, anyway, Jane? Was she real or an imaginary character?

JANE: Barbara Frietchie was supposed to have been real, but

there are plenty of doubts about that today. She is supposed to have lived in Frederick, Md. And when Stonewall Jackson and his army marched through the town during the Civil War, people say that she defiantly waved the Stars and Stripes from her window.

ALICE: I wouldn't call her much of a heroine. Any other woman could have done the same thing and gotten away with it, if Jackson was the kind of a gentleman we've been taught that he was.

JANE: I don't doubt that a bit. But when I think of the great women our nation has produced, I think of Mary Lyon, who began her school teaching days at a salary of seventy-five cents a day; even when she began Mount Holyoke Female Seminary, she never received over $200 a year. I call her a heroine of the first order. Our nation could do with a few less Barbara Frietchies and a few more Mary Lyons.

ALICE: And we all say "Amen" to that. I'd like to recommend for our hall of fame Susan B. Anthony, our advocate of woman's suffrage. It's coming some day; probably not within our lifetime, but it is coming, and when it does, hers will be the glory and the honor.

MARY: And I'd put up the name of our scientist, Maria Mitchell, our oustanding woman astronomer from Vassar.

MISS BATES: And what of Emma Willard and Frances Willard and the hosts of other women who are giving their lives to the making of an educated, enlightened, clean, sober America? They are our heroes, proved in liberating strife. They are as willing to give their lives over a period of years, as are the soldiers who are willing to give their lives in a moment of battle. We need them both. Let us never forget it. I want my third stanza to honor those heroes who are willing to LIVE for their country, to help God refine America's gold, till her greatest success is her nobleness, till her every gain is divinely approved and divinely blessed!

ALICE: Did you say the last stanza would be about patriots?

MISS BATES: Yes; I want to honor our far-seeing patriots who plan for the years ahead, instead of the short-sighted ones who can only think of their own pocketbooks and what they can get out of the country.

MARY: I thought about that when we attended the exposition. It took a lot of planning and far-sightedness on the part of Daniel Burnham to design those remarkable groups of buildings. I understand that several cities are already planning to appoint some of their leaders to lay out designs for future expansion, along the lines of the exposition structures and plans. That is far-seeing patriotism.

MISS BATES: Do any of you remember the glistening alabaster we saw from Pike's Peak, the shining reflections in the sun from the distant hills and surrounding peaks?

ALICE: Why, yes. What about it?

MISS BATES: I like to think of God putting all that dazzling beauty there to remind us that He wants all of His cities to gleam like alabaster and He wants all of His people to live their lives undimmed by human tears.

JANE: "Undimmed by human tears." That is a beautiful line, Katharine. I wonder if the world will ever see such a city. No more tears from children's eyes, when fathers and mothers neglect them shamefully. No more tears in the youthful eyes of those who cannot find work or who have to work such long hours they never have time to play.

MARY: And no more tears in the eyes of fathers and mothers, when their sons are forced to fight in futile wars, some never to return home again. No more tears in the eyes of mothers whose homes are broken by the liquor traffic, monuments to the greed and selfishness of unredeemed humanity.

MISS BATES: We must tie up our dreams for the future America with Jesus' dreams of the present reality of God's Kingdom. Only then can God "wipe away all tears" from their eyes.

JANE (*rising suddenly*): Well, come on, girls; it's time for bed. If we expect to do any teaching tomorrow, we'd better get to bed early.

(*The other two girls rise and get ready to leave the room.*)

MARY: Katharine, don't try to do too much tonight. Remember, you went along with us today, and we have an idea how tired you really are.

MISS BATES (*getting up, walking toward the door with her*

friends): I promise that I'll retire within half an hour. Is that all right?

ALICE: Good. But be sure to keep your promise. I know how you poets are. You're liable to get so wrapped up in your work that we'll find you here tomorrow morning when we come to breakfast.

MISS BATES: I doubt that. Now, run along and get some sleep. We have a busy day ahead of us. Goodnight—goodnight—

(*The three teachers bid her "Goodnight" in turn, and exit through door at the right. After they have gone, MISS BATES returns to her table, goes over her writings, picks up a clean sheet of paper, and begins writing the last two stanzas of her poem. As she writes down the lines, reading them aloud as she does so, OFF-STAGE CHORUS hums the music of the hymn tune MATERNA, by Ward, synchronizing the music with her words, so humming the tune twice gives her ample time to complete the last two stanzas of her poem. (AN ORGANIST may play the music, in place of the CHORUS, if a choral group is unavailable.) As MISS BATES reads her stanzas, the lights in the room are gradually dimmed, and a spotlight focused on her is brightened, until, at the close of the scene, all lights are out save the brilliant light of the spotlight, offstage, focused on her.*)

MISS BATES (*reading her lines with much feeling, as she writes*):

> O beautiful for heroes proved
> In liberating strife;
> Who more than self their country loved,
> And mercy more than life;
> America! America!
> May God thy gold refine;
> Till all success is nobleness,
> And every gain divine.
>
> O beautiful for patriot dream
> That sees beyond the years
> Thine alabaster cities gleam
> Undimmed by human tears.
> America! America!

God shed His grace on thee;
And crown thy good with brotherhood
From sea to shining sea.[1]

(CURTAIN *closes on the scene, as* MISS BATES *remains reverently seated at the table.* OFF-STAGE CHORUS *sings, full voice, the first stanza of this hymn; or* ORGANIST *plays it with full organ.*)

NARRATOR (*center stage, in front of curtain*): The stanzas of this new patriotic hymn did not appear in print until two years after they were written. In "The Congregationalist" of July 4, 1895, they appeared for the first time outside of the author's notebook. The response of the American people to her stanzas was immediate; they were accepted, quoted, and widely acclaimed. Of the many musical settings, only one has endured to the present, the tune "Materna" which Samuel A. Ward wrote for the hymn "O Mother Dear, Jerusalem"; and today this hymn and that tune are wedded in the hearts and minds of the American people. Miss Bates was honored with many degrees from many leading universities and colleges; from her prolific pen seventeen books flowed. She retired as professor at Wellesley, after forty-five years of teaching, in 1925, when she became professor-emeritus. Four years later she passed away at Wellesley, on March 29, 1929.

The first outstanding patriotic hymn in our history came from the pen of a young lawyer, Francis Scott Key, who wrote "The Star-Spangled Banner" in 1814; the second popularly acclaimed patriotic hymn was written by a young Baptist minister, Samuel Francis Smith, who wrote "My Country, 'tis of Thee" in 1832. It is fitting that our third great patriotic hymn should come from the pen of an educator, an outstanding college professor, a Christian woman, Katharine Lee Bates. As long as the court, the Church and the school support and defend our American freedoms, we have nothing to fear in the future!

(NARRATOR *may invite the assembled congregation to sing this entire hymn in closing, if appropriate. Otherwise, exit* NARRATOR.)

[1] The poem, "America The Beautiful," is used with permission of the executors of the poet's estate, which controls the copyright, Mr. and Mrs. George Sargent Burgess.

(Note: *If no curtain is available, the play may begin as* MISS BATES *enters the room and sits at her desk; it may close as she finishes her poem, stands a moment in silence, extinguishes the light, and quietly exits.*)

BATTLE HYMN OF THE REPUBLIC

1861

BATTLE HYMN OF THE REPUBLIC

6 men
2 women
Male Quartet

CHARACTERS

WILLIAM STEFFE, in his late twenties; pianist, soloist, song-leader.
FRANCIS and GEORGE, about the same age; his friends and fellow-musicians.
MALE QUARTET of young soldiers from Second Battalion of Massachusetts' Infantry.
MRS. JULIA WARD HOWE, 42; cultured, gracious, Christian woman.
DR. SAMUEL GRIDLEY HOWE, her husband, twenty years her senior.
REV. JAMES FREEMAN CLARKE, her pastor; middle-aged.
MRS. CLARKE, his wife.
NARRATOR.

> Costumes and interior for scene 1, typical of the rural Deep South about 1856; for scene 2, typical of cultured and well-to-do Washington, D.C., 1861.

Scene 1

SETTING: A simple, plainly furnished room, in a semi-dormitory on the ground of a southern Camp Meeting. Plain chairs, a table or two, simple cots, plain curtains on the windows, and other period rustic furniture complete the camp-like atmosphere. An old reed organ, or a piano, is against the left side of the room; the door is at the right. As the scene opens, MR. STEFFE is seated in the middle of the room, reading a small book, The Methodist Discipline, 1784 edition. The State, Georgia.

TIME: One afternoon, about 4 o'clock; the early summer of 1856.

NARRATOR (*center stage, in front of curtain*): The first scene of this play takes place in the room occupied by Mr. William Steffe, Richmond, Virginia song-leader and musician, on the grounds of a Georgia Camp Meeting where he is in charge of the music. Associated with him are two of his friends and fellow-musicians, known to us as Francis and George. It is about 4 o'clock one afternoon in the early summer of 1856. As the scene opens, we find Mr. Steffe in his room, reading.

(*Exit* NARRATOR.)

(*Curtain is raised, revealing scene described above.* MR. STEFFE *continues reading the book in his hands, pausing at times to refer to other pages, sometimes bursting into laughter at what he reads. After a few moments, he calls through the nearby window.*)

MR. STEFFE: Francis— Oh, Francis—are you out there?

FRANCIS (*off-stage left*): Right here, William. What is it?

MR. STEFFE: Come in a minute, will you? I just found something here that ought to interest you.

FRANCIS (*off-stage*): Coming. (*He enters a moment later through the door at the right, and walks over to where* MR. STEFFE *is reading, in the center of the room, speaking as he does.*) Here I am. What is it?

MR. STEFFE (*looking up, motioning to a nearby chair*): Pull up a chair and lend me your ear.

FRANCIS (*pulling a chair close and sitting down*): Sounds Shakespearean—what is it?

MR. STEFFE: Is it true that you want to be a Methodist minister?

FRANCIS: That's the general idea—that is, if the Conference will have me. Why?

MR. STEFFE (*laughing*): You mean if you will have the Conference. Listen to this. (*He reads from the volume in his hands.*) "Let the women constantly sing their parts alone. Let no man sing with them—unless he understands the notes and sings the bass, and it is printed down in the book— Introduce no new tunes till they are perfect in the old—let no organs be placed anywhere till proposed in Conference— Recommend our tune book everywhere—and if you cannot sing yourself, choose a person or two in each place to pitch the tune for you—"

FRANCIS: Just what is that, William?

MR. STEFFE (*showing him the book*): The Methodist Discipline of 1784, in which brother John Wesley laid down the rules for you boys to obey—or else!

FRANCIS: It can't be that bad. (*He reads further on the same page.*) "Exhort everyone in the congregation to sing, not one in ten only—"

MR. STEFFE: He knew his Methodists, didn't he?

FRANCIS: You're right, there. (*Reading.*) "Do not suffer people to sing too slow. This naturally tends to formality and is brought in by them who have either very strong or very weak voices." (*Looking up.*) Say, he knew quite a good deal about congregational singing, didn't he?

MR. STEFFE: He ought to. He started the Church and gave the rules for her continued operation. And that, brother, included a knowledge of music and congregational singing.

FRANCIS: Then I'd better thank my lucky stars that I know a little about music.

MR. STEFFE: You're right, there, brother. (*Taking the book and reading further.*) Look at this, Francis. This is the best part of the whole business. (*Reading aloud.*) "After preaching, take a little lemonade, mild ale or candied orange-peel. All spiritous liquors are deadly poison."

FRANCIS: He's still right, as far as that's concerned. What else does he say?

MR. STEFFE (*reading further*): He asks a question: "Are there any smaller advices relative to preaching which might be of use to us?" And gives this answer: "Sing no hymns of your own composing."

FRANCIS: Didn't that cramp his brother Charles' style? After all, he wrote most of the Methodist hymns, and if his congregation were prohibited from singing them, they must have been in a bad way.

MR. STEFFE: Maybe he ordered a special version of the discipline for Charles, with that line eliminated.

FRANCIS: If John had been my brother, he'd have eliminated that, or else I might have eliminated him.

(*Off-stage left,* GEORGE *calls and* FRANCIS *goes to the door to reply.*)

GEORGE: William, are you in?

FRANCIS (*at the door, calling off-stage*): Right here, George. Come on over.

(*Enter* GEORGE *through door at right, carrying a volume with him.*)

MR. STEFFE: Come on in, George. What's that you're reading?

GEORGE (*showing him the book, as he and* FRANCIS *take chairs near the center of the room*): Wesley's Journal.

FRANCIS: You too? We were just going over his rules for singing, in the old Discipline. Boy, he really had those early Methodists going.

GEORGE: Judging by his Journal he did a heap of going himself. How about it, William?

MR. STEFFE: Right you are, George. He had to, to keep his new churches alive and growing. It's a miracle the whole thing didn't collapse when he died. If he hadn't organized the thing so magnificently, it would have.

GEORGE (*pointing out a passage in the Journal*): Read that, William. It'll do Francis good, if he's still planning to be a Methodist preacher.

FRANCIS: Read it, William; you've got my curiosity aroused.

MR. STEFFE (*reading from the Journal*): It's about some of Wesley's experiences with his early congregations. Listen to this: "The service was at the usual hour. I came in just in time to put a stop to a bad custom which was creeping in here; a few men who had fine voices, sung a psalm which no one knew, in a tune fit for an opera."

FRANCIS: He had that down pat. I've heard enough of those tunes myself.

MR. STEFFE (*continuing his reading*): "Three, four or five persons sung different words at the same time. What an insult upon common sense. What a burlesque upon public worship. No custom can excuse such a mixture of profaneness and absurdity."

GEORGE: I wonder how Mr. Wesley and Mr. Handel would have gotten along with Mr. Handel's Messiah with its fugues and counterpoint and what not?

FRANCIS: Badly, I'm afraid. The old fellow wouldn't have given Handel any peace.

MR. STEFFE (*reading further*): Here's another one. "At Neath I began to read prayers at six, but was greatly disgusted at the manner of singing; twelve or fourteen persons kept it to themselves, and quite shut out the congregation; these repeated the same words contrary to all sense and reason, six, eight or ten times over; according to the shocking custom of modern music, different persons sung different words at one and the same moment, an intolerable insult on common sense and utterly incompatible with any devotion."

FRANCIS: Well, that's that. All modern music may be henceforth ruled out of Methodism.

GEORGE: Oh, I don't believe he meant it that way. He was criticizing those congregations that turn over all their singing to a paid few in the choir, and who miss the joy of singing themselves.

MR. STEFFE: I think that was it, George. Surely he would have been inspired by the Hallelujah Chorus, as we are today, in spite of its difficult music and voices singing different words at the same time.

FRANCIS: But he did have something there, about congregational singing being so limited. I wonder why that is?

MR. STEFFE: Look at the hymns we have today. Impossible, most of them.

FRANCIS: Not as impossible as some Charles Wesley wrote. After all, some of his poetry is pretty deep and pretty heavy for the average congregation.

GEORGE: I'll grant you that, Francis; but he had one advantage over us.

FRANCIS: What was that?

GEORGE: He had class meetings for his people, and in those regular weekly meetings the people could be taught those stanzas by heart; in a few months, they'd know about all the hymns necessary for worship, and then never need a hymnal.

MR. STEFFE: That's an interesting observation, George. I never thought of it just that way before. But Isaac Watts wrote great poetry, too. And just how many of our Methodists down in the South sing his hymns today?

FRANCIS: Very few—too few—and I'll tell you why. It's because he wrote most of his hymns for the formal High Church-

men, and not for the average run of uneducated and uncultured tenant farmers.

GEORGE: If they could be touched up with a good chorus—

MR. STEFFE: That's what we need right here in this meeting, a good rousing chorus or two— A song-leader can always sing the verses if the congregation will join in the chorus—

GEORGE: Did Watts or Wesley ever write choruses for their hymns?

FRANCIS: Hardly ever. I always think of a hymn as a song of praise without a chorus, and a song as a song of praise with a chorus.

MR. STEFFE (*laughing*): Good boy, Francis. Keep it up and you'll really make a contribution to religious music some of these days.

FRANCIS: But, William, all joking aside, isn't that one reason for the poor singing in our churches? Turning the singing over to a paid and highly trained choir—writing all our music on that level—eliminating rousing, and even swingy choruses, because the highly trained choir objects—and the first thing you know the very choir you employed to help your church music ends up by doing it more damage than good!

MR. STEFFE: Well, Francis, "St. Anne" is a great tune, and it has no refrain.

FRANCIS: I know that; but we can't be singing "St. Anne" all the time. Sometimes we want a light, swingy, easy and simple tune, so everyone can join in, even the tiny children—

GEORGE: Almost like a Negro spiritual. Is that what you mean?

FRANCIS: Exactly. Now take one of those spirituals. What does it have? Two things: repetition, and simplicity. They sing the same line over and over again, to a melody that a child can learn—and soon the entire congregation is swept along with the unity and fire of the music—all join in because all *can* join in—it's the kind of a song that has a heart appeal, a head appeal, and a voice appeal—

GEORGE: And a foot appeal!

FRANCIS (*laughing*): All right. Even foot appeal. And I like to tap my foot to good rhythm as much as you. There's nothing ungodly in good rhythm, is there?

MR. STEFFE (*going over to the reed organ*): Nothing at all, Francis. I like it myself—and I think everyone else does, whether they admit it or not.

GEORGE: And you mean, Francis, that if we could combine all of those elements, we could really produce a hit hymn?

FRANCIS: I never heard a hymn called a hit before, but it might as well be called a hit as some of the ditties the folks sing all the time, because they are hits. Am I right, William?

MR. STEFFE (*at the piano, or organ, picking out a melody or two*): I believe so, Francis. I was just thinking over some of the spirituals—"Swing Low, Sweet Chariot"—"Standing in the Need of Prayer"—"Little David"—"Go Down, Moses"—

FRANCIS (*going to his side*): Lots of repetition and simplicity, isn't there?

MR. STEFFE: Yes, there is.

FRANCIS (*as GEORGE rises and joins them by the piano*): And if we could combine the dignity of Watts and Wesley with the simplicity and repetition of the spiritual, we'd really have it, wouldn't we?

MR. STEFFE (*picking out a melody*): I suppose so. But don't forget that heart appeal of yours . . .

GEORGE: And that foot appeal.

FRANCIS: All right. Let's get all those appeals, and then save money by not having to print hymn books, since folks could memorize the song when we taught it to them.

GEORGE: The churches would agree, though the publishing agents might raise a howl.

MR. STEFFE: Back to that song Francis. How should it go? I mean, what theme would you choose?

FRANCIS: Well, the people here surely love Watts' "There Is a Land of Pure Delight, Where Saints Immortal Reign."

GEORGE: Folks always want to sing about heaven. It has that heart appeal. Especially when they have brothers or sisters or loved ones up there.

FRANCIS: All right, use that theme. Say, brothers, will you meet us— Say, brothers, will you meet us—

GEORGE: "On Jordan's stormy banks"—they love that down here—

FRANCIS (*as MR. STEFFE picks out a melody, the same one*

to which we sing "The Battle Hymn of the Republic" today): Change "Jordan" to something else.

GEORGE: On Canaan's shore—Holy Land—Palestine—land of milk and honey—

FRANCIS: No—you had it in "Canaan"—on Canaan's pleasant shore—blissful shore—

˙GEORGE: They have a hymn with blissful shore, I think.

FRANCIS: Well, make it "Canaan's happy shore"—that's original enough, isn't it?

GEORGE: Suits me. How about you, William?

MR. STEFFE (*still playing over his melody, the simplified melody to which "The Battle Hymn of the Republic" is sung today*): If you'll give me three lines and a chorus we'll have it.

FRANCIS: George, write these words down, will you? We might forget them before tonight.

GEORGE (*getting paper and pencil, sitting down at a table and taking down the words*): Tonight? Are you really going to introduce the song tonight, William?

MR. STEFFE: Why not? If it's a hit, why keep it from the world; and if it's not, the sooner we know it the better for the world.

GEORGE: Fair enough. All set, Francis?

FRANCIS: Say, brothers will you meet us,— You want it repeated three times, William?

MR. STEFFE (*playing the melody*): Yes; it'll suit my tune better.

FRANCIS: All right. Got it George?

Say, brothers, will you meet us,
Say, brothers, will you meet us,
Say, brothers, will you meet us,
On Canaan's happy shore?

MR. STEFFE: Francis, if we can use the same melodic line for the chorus, it would be even better.

GEORGE: Don't forget the "Hallelujahs" and the "Glorys," Francis. The folks will eat them up, if I know these Methodists.

FRANCIS: Well, let's have it:

Glory, glory Hallelujah,
Glory, glory Hallelujah,
Glory, glory Hallelujah,
For ever, evermore!

MR. STEFFE: Good. That fits the music—the melody—let me see how it sounds. Here goes. (*He plays and sings the first stanza and chorus to his new music; the others nod in enthusiastic approval as he sings. When he finishes, they burst into applause, and congratulate him.*) Oh, it's not much. Chances are it will die before the summer is out.

GEORGE: And if it doesn't, and becomes famous, some prominent composer will claim that he thought of it first, and then we'll be back where we started from—

FRANCIS: That's not worrying me. I hope it goes over tonight—we expect a big crowd—one of the bishops is coming down to preach—

GEORGE: Well, boys, it better be good, or I'm liable to find myself kept out of the Conference for good. Now, what about a second verse, Francis? What do you say?

MR. STEFFE: Go on. It's all right with me.

FRANCIS: By the grace of God we'll meet you,
By the grace of God we'll meet you,
By the grace of God we'll meet you,
On Canaan's happy shore.

MR. STEFFE: Change the last line, Francis. How about, "Where parting is no more"?

FRANCIS: Better. Put that down, George.

GEORGE: Got it; now one more, and we're through. Can't we put in some extra verses about, "Say, sister, will you meet us?"; and for tonight we can slip in a verse about, "Say, bishop, will you meet us?"

FRANCIS: Nothing doing. Always end a hymn on a high plane, with praise to God and to the Son. We could sing this:

Jesus lives and reigns forever,
Jesus lives and reigns forever,
Jesus lives and reigns forever,
On Canaan's happy shore.

181

And then the chorus about "Glory, glory Hallelujah." How's that?

MR. STEFFE: Good enough for me. We'll try it out tonight and see how the public reacts. Fellows, before we get ready for supper, let's try it out together. George, put the words on the piano.

GEORGE (*taking the words and placing the paper on the piano as the three prepare to sing*): The world premiere—is that good English, Francis?

FRANCIS: It sounds dignified enough for a new opera or an oratorio. And a bit too high-class for a Georgia Camp Meeting song.

MR. STEFFE: Ready, boys. Let's go.

(*As MR. STEFFE plays the music, full chords, the three join in singing the first stanza and chorus, with fervor and feeling. As they finish the last lines of the chorus, the curtain closes on the scene.*)

NARRATOR (*center stage in front of curtain, as the stage is being set for scene 2*): Within a few years' time, the melody of this new camp meeting song reached the New England states, through travelling preachers, visiting musicians, and the usual strange methods that popular songs have of getting from place to place. By the time the Civil War broke, early in 1861, the music was known in Massachusetts. There, the Second Battalion of Massachusetts' Infantry was ordered to occupy and prepare for defense, Fort Warren, in Boston Harbor. The glee club, and male quartet of this group of young men, were already familiar with the Georgia song, and used its melody to lighten the hours of hard physical labor in repairing and improving the defenses of the Fort. But let the quartet speak for itself.

(*Exit NARRATOR.*)

(MALE QUARTET *of young soldiers, dressed as the "Yankee" soldiers of 1861, comes on stage, in front of curtain, and their spokesman introduces them.*)

SPOKESMAN: There is a Scotchman in our group who is named John Brown. Now, he is absolutely no kin to the John Brown who raided Harpers Ferry in 1859. But, since the names were exactly the same, we decided to get up a good joke on our John Brown, by writing a song about him, to be sung to that

"Glory Hallelujah" song that some of the boys brought up from a Georgia camp meeting. Of course the poets in our company have written all sorts of verses to the music since we prepared our own original stanzas, but we will sing for you the song as we prepared it, in this, the first year of the Civil War, up in Massachusetts.

(*The* MALE QUARTET *then sings the "John Brown Song," using these six stanzas and chorus; and the Battle Hymn of the Republic music*):

1. John Brown's body lies a-mouldering in the grave,
   John Brown's body lies a-mouldering in the grave,
   John Brown's body lies a-mouldering in the grave,
   His soul goes marching on!
   CHORUS: Glory, glory hallelujah; glory, glory hal-
   lelujah,
   Glory, glory hallelujah, His soul goes
   marching on!

2. He's gone to be a soldier in the army of the Lord
   (repeat twice)
   His soul goes marching on!
   CHORUS:

3. John Brown's knapsack is strapped upon his back
   (repeat twice)
   His soul goes marching on!
   CHORUS:

4. His pet lambs will meet him on the way (repeat
   twice)
   As they go marching on!
   CHORUS:

5. They'll hang Jeff Davis to a sour apple tree (repeat
   twice)
   As they go marching on!
   CHORUS:

6. Now for the Union we will give three rousing cheers
   (repeat twice)
   As they go marching on!
   CHORUS:

(When they finish singing, Exit MALE QUARTET.)

NARRATOR *(center stage, in front of curtain)*: This second
battalion, nicknamed "The Tigers," was not accepted as an
independent military unit by the government, whereupon many
of the men enlisted in the Twelfth Massachusetts Regiment,
commanded by Colonel Fletcher Webster. When this regiment
marched across Boston Common, en route from Fort Warren to
the Providence depot, to entrain for New York, they sang the
"John Brown Song"; again while marching down Broadway,
in New York City, they sang it, and the people took up the
strains with wild enthusiasm. So from Georgia, in the deep
South, to Massachusetts, in the deep North, the song sang its
way into the hearts of all who heard it, awaiting the hour when
a gifted poet would add fitting stanzas to its lilting melody,
and give to the Republic another great stirring, timeless, patriotic hymn. Where could that take place in a more appropriate
setting than the capital city, Washington, D.C.?

(Exit NARRATOR, *as* OFF-STAGE, *the* MALE QUARTET
sings the chorus of "John Brown's" song, softly.)

Scene 2

SETTING: A hotel room in the two-room suite in the Willard Hotel,
Washington, D.C. occupied by Dr. and Mrs. Howe. The room may be
basically the same as that used in scene 1, only with better furniture,
more expensive decorations, draperies, rugs, pictures and other pieces
of period furniture. This is primarily a sitting room, with desk, table,
bookcases, comfortable chairs, etc.; the bedroom adjoins, with the door
at the right of the stage. Two windows look out from back stage. The
setting is comfortable, despite the hardships of the war period. As the
scene opens, no one is in the room.

TIME: Late one night, December, 1861.

NARRATOR *(center stage, in front of curtain)*: Julia Ward
was born on May 27, 1819, the daughter of a wealthy banker,
and distinguished citizen, Samuel Ward. Early her literary gifts
were evident in the prolific writings of her school days. In 1843
she married Dr. Samuel Gridley Howe, head of the Perkins
Institute for the Blind; they honeymooned in Europe, meeting
many distinguished literary and political people. Returning
home, they both became very active in the abolitionist move-

ment, counting among their friends William Lloyd Garrison and Wendell Phillips. Too old for military service when the Civil War broke, Dr. Howe accepted a position with the Sanitary Commission of the government, and used his skill as a physician to render assistance to those wounded in battle. Thus it was that he and his wife were in Washington, D.C., occupying rooms in the Willard Hotel, in December of 1861. This scene takes place late one night of that month and year, in their hotel suite. It is Mrs. Howe's forty-second year.

(*Exit* NARRATOR.)

(*Curtain is raised, revealing the scene described above. After a moment, voices of* DR. *and* MRS. HOWE *and* REV. MR. *and* MRS. CLARKE. *The door opens, and* MRS. HOWE *enters, followed by her husband and their friends. Coats and wraps are removed and laid over a nearby chair.* MRS. HOWE *shows her guests to comfortable chairs, as their conversation continues.*)

DR. HOWE: That was a thrilling sight—thrilling—

REV. MR. CLARKE: If it wasn't to be so tragic—so tragic—when I think of those handsome young men—their wives—their homes—

MRS. HOWE: And their mothers and sweethearts—

MRS. CLARKE: But weren't they enthusiastic—it's so strange—

MRS. HOWE: Young men are always enthusiastic when they march off to war—it's when they return that you see the horror of it in their eyes—

DR. HOWE: And in their minds—the shock—the horror—the blood—

REV. MR. CLARKE: But don't you think our men can finish this thing up in a few weeks?

MRS. HOWE: If only they could, but I doubt it—

DR. HOWE: That's why the young men were so enthusiastic —they actually think they can whip the Confederates in six weeks—if they knew that the war wouldn't end in six weeks or even six months—

MRS. CLARKE: Dr. Howe, do you really believe it will last six months—I can't believe it—six more months—after almost a year—

REV. MR. CLARKE: Or six years?

185

MRS. HOWE: If it lasted six months or six years or even four years, those young men wouldn't have marched as valiantly and bravely as they did tonight—if they knew the struggle was to bog down into a bloody slaughter, they would be the first to demand some other solution to this problem—

REV. MR. CLARKE: But the irony of it all is that the ones who have to fight never have the right to say whether war shall be declared or not—they just do the fighting and the dying and some other men—

MR. HOWE: Older men, too, not young men—

REV. MR. CLARKE: You're right—some older men bungle another peace and the vicious circle begins again—

DR. HOWE: Continues, you mean, as it has been continuing since Cain slew his brother Abel.

MRS. HOWE: That sense of futility overcomes me—obsesses me—and sometimes makes me feel so depressed—

REV. MR. CLARKE: Then why don't you concentrate on that poem I asked you to write earlier this evening?

MRS. HOWE: That "John Brown's Body" one?

REV. MR. CLARKE: Yes. Governor Andrew was impressed with the idea, and I still think it is good, even if the original suggestion did come from me!

MRS. CLARKE: And I agree, Mrs. Howe. Everyone in the service knows that tune—if only some stirring words could be written, it would sweep the country like a wild fire—

DR. HOWE: And give us all an extra shot in the arm—

REV. MR. CLARKE: Or the heart, where we need it most—

MRS. HOWE: But you can't order up a poem like you order a meal at a restaurant or groceries down at the grocery store.

REV. MR. CLARKE: I don't know about that, Mrs. Howe. Don't forget that the song the South is singing now, that "Dixie," was ordered by the owner of that minstrel show Dan Emmett travelled with—and it didn't turn out so badly, did it?

MRS. HOWE: But this is different—I'm no entertainer—no famous black-faced minstrel star—

REV. MR. CLARKE: All the more reason why you should write that song—maybe that's the trouble with our patriotic songs. We've turned over the field to entertainers and comedians and

186

funny men in funny costumes who do funny dances and tell silly stories—

MRS. CLARKE: And remember it was a young minister who wrote "My Country 'Tis of Thee" and that will live long after that "Dixie" song is forgotten—

DR. HOWE: And wasn't Francis Scott Key a lawyer? Every school boy knows that.

MRS. HOWE: But I'm the wife—and the satisfied and happy wife—of an army physician—I don't think that calls for any special creative efforts on my part, does it, since Samuel is doing all the patriotic work this family can afford to do right now?

DR. HOWE: But I'm not a poet, Julia. If I were, I would be carving words instead of people—

REV. MR. CLARKE: Or splitting infinitives instead of flesh and bones?

DR. HOWE: Maybe so— But you know, I was looking forward to that review today. I knew many of the men who were going to take part.

REV. MR. CLARKE: I wonder why the enemy chose this particular day for his surprise attack?

MRS. CLARKE: His spies told him, no doubt. It's like a fireman's banquet when the biggest fire of the year breaks out, and no one is there to fight it—

MRS. HOWE: Or the policeman's ball, when the biggest robbery of the year takes place—

REV. MR. CLARKE: That may be it, seriously. We've underestimated the shrewdness of our enemy, I believe. He is smart, crafty and quite courageous, else he wouldn't have dared an assault like today's.

MRS. CLARKE: And if you hadn't started singing "John Brown's Body," those poor fellows would have run all the way back to the city—then what would have happened?

DR. HOWE: Possibly a siege of Washington, and the war not a year old yet.

MRS. CLARKE: Could the city hold out, Doctor?

DR. HOWE: More than likely. Reinforcements are not too far away—and supplies from Baltimore and Philadelphia could reach us as quickly as supplies from Richmond could reach them—it might be a tug of war—but I think we'd win—

REV. MR. CLARKE (*rising, getting his wraps*): Well, dear, we must be going. It's late—we've had such an exciting time of it—and you must be tired, Doctor, after all that work—

DR. HOWE (*rising, helping the* CLARKES *with their wraps*): Thank you for coming home with us—we will try to be out for the morning worship Sunday morning— Goodnight—(*He shakes hands with them both.* MRS. HOWE *rises, and bids her guests goodnight, and they both walk to the door with them.*)

REV. MR. CLARKE: Now, don't forget that song, Mrs. Howe. I'll be expecting to hear about it before very long.

MRS. HOWE: I'll do my best, but don't expect too much, please.

MRS. CLARKE: It's been a pleasant evening. Do come and see us some evening when neither of us will be occupied with pastoral work or war duties. We'd love to have you both.

REV. MR. CLARKE: About that song. You remember that during the Revolutionary War, William Billings wrote his famous "Battle Hymn of the Revolution"?

DR. HOWE: How well I do. I had to memorize it in school. I think I can recall the first stanza now:

> "Let tyrants shake their iron rod,
> And slavery clank her galling chains:
> We see them not; We trust in God:
> New England's God forever reigns."

REV. MR. CLARKE: Good—good— Now the Civil War ought to have its own battle song—something of a Battle Hymn for the Republic.

MRS. HOWE: Thank you for the suggestion. Goodnight. (*They shake hands, give their farewells. Exit* REV. MR. CLARKE *and* MRS. CLARKE *through door at right.* MRS. HOWE *goes back to the table, picks up a book, sits down in an easy chair to browse through the pages.* DR. HOWE *goes over to the window, looks out over the city, down at the street below. After a few minutes,* MRS. HOWE *walks over to his side.*)

DR. HOWE (*pointing at the street outside the window*): There they go now—a fine couple—I enjoy them both—

MRS. HOWE: You know, Samuel, I ought to write a poem, just to humor Mr. Clarke. He seemed so insistent—almost too much so—

DR. HOWE: Dear, your singing did stop what might have been a calamitous retreat. The spirit of the boys went up a thousand percent when you burst into that "John Brown's Body" song.

MRS. HOWE: Oh, Samuel, the boys were just tired. Singing gave them a needed lift in spirits—boosted their morale—anyone else could have done it far more effectively—

DR. HOWE (*pointing out over the distant city*): Look, Julia —look at that marvelous sight—

MRS. HOWE (*peering through the window*): My—almost like a distant scene in a novel—there must be a hundred—a thousand of those tiny campfires all around the city—

DR. HOWE: And as long as they are there, we are safe—you can almost hear the bugles blowing taps—(*Way in the distance a faint note of a bugle is heard.*)— Listen—there it is—a trumpet sound—

MRS. HOWE: That shall never call retreat— Glory, glory Hallelujah, Our God is marching on—

DR. HOWE: That will make a majestic chorus, Julia.

MRS. HOWE: For what?

DR. HOWE: Brother Clarke's new hymn.

MRS. HOWE: Samuel, stop teasing—there isn't going to be any Clarke hymn, now or any other time.

DR. HOWE: Then why did you promise—

MRS. HOWE: To humor him—that's positively why I promised—

DR. HOWE: I'm going to bed—and I'm going to leave you here all by yourself—if that view from the window—and that sight—and the memories of all that occurred today can't give you any poetic inspiration—I've misjudged my wife's talents—

MRS. HOWE: You have, Samuel—and if you rate me too high, it's not my fault—only your own.

DR. HOWE (*crossing the room to the door*): Goodnight, Julia. I'll be hearing from you, in the morning.

Mrs. Howe: Goodnight, dear. If I write anything, it will be to pacify Dr. Clarke, and not to try to rise to my husband's expectations.

(*Exit* Dr. Howe. Mrs. Howe *picks up a sheet of paper and a pencil, walks over to the window and looks out over the silent city, surrounded by the camps of the soldiers. In the distance the* Male Quartet *sings, very softly, the refrain "Glory, glory Hallelujah." Then, as she begins to write down her stanzas, reading them aloud as she writes,* Male Quartet *hums the music of her hymn, synchronizing the music so that humming the tune three times will give her sufficient time to write down the 5 stanzas and choruses of her hymn. The lights gradually are dimmed, and a spotlight shines on* Mrs. Howe, *growing brighter and brighter, until, at the final chorus, the room is dark, and the light on her glows with full brilliance. She stands by the window, so as to be partly facing the audience, yet able to see outside.*)

Mrs. Howe (*writing, reading her stanzas with fervor and feeling as she does so*):

Mine eyes have seen the glory of the coming of the
    Lord;
He is trampling out the vintage where the grapes of
    wrath are stored;
He hath loosed the fateful lightning of his terrible
    swift sword,
His truth is marching on.

I have seen him in the watch-fires of a hundred cir-
    cling camps;
They have builded him an altar in the evening dews
    and damps;
I can read his righteous sentence by the dim and flaring
    lamps;
His day is marching on.

I have read a fiery gospel, writ in burnished rows of
    steel:

"As ye deal with my contemners, so with you my
   grace shall deal;
Let the Hero, born of woman, crush the serpent with
   his heel";
Our God is marching on.

He has sounded forth the trumpet that shall never call
   retreat;
He is sifting out the hearts of men before his judgment seat;
So be swift, my soul, to answer him, be jubilant my
   feet!
Our God is marching on.

In the beauty of the lilies Christ was born across the
   sea,
With a glory in his bosom that transfigures you and
   me;
As he died to make men holy, let us die to make men
   free,
While God is marching on.

Glory, glory, Hallelujah, glory, glory, Hallelujah,
Glory, glory, Hallelujah; Our God is marching on!

(*As she repeats the refrain, and the music comes to a close, the
curtain closes on the scene.*)

NARRATOR (*center stage, in front of curtain*): Sent to the
Atlantic Monthly magazine, this poem was published in the
issue of February 1862, and was immediately accepted as
the battle song of the Republic for the Civil War. During
the intervening years, it has lost none of its fire, although the
immediate cause for which it was written has long since been
practically forgotten. As the South took for its fighting song
"Dixie," written by a northern boy in New York City, so the
North took for its fighting song a melody that originally came
from a Georgia camp meeting. Maybe when Sherman made his
famous march to the sea, the soldiers sang this song, and the

Georgians, thinking it was a group going to camp meeting, merely stepped aside, and he marched on through! The author enjoyed many honors and was awarded many degrees by colleges and universities. She passed away in her ninety-first year, at her home near Newport, Rhode Island, October 17, 1910, "marching to brave music still."

(*Exit* NARRATOR.)